The
PEOPLE Approach
to Customer Service

by Carl Henry

© 2008 Carl Henry. All rights reserved. Printed and bound in the United States of America. No part of this book my be reproduced or transmitted in any form or by any means, electronic or mechanical, including photocopying, recording, or by an information storage and retrieval system – except by a reviewer who may quote brief passages in a review to be printed in a magazine, newspaper, or on the Web – without permission in writing from the author. For information, please contact Henry Associates, 9430 Valley Road, Charlotte, NC 28270.

Cover Design by Alex LaFasto
Book design by Nichole Ward, Morrison Alley Design

Although the author and publisher have made every effort to ensure the accuracy and completeness of information contained in this book, we assume no responsibility for errors, inaccuracies, omissions, or any inconsistency herein. Any slights of people, places, or organizations are unintentional.

First Printing 2008

ISBN 978-0-9817915-0-0

HELPING BUILD SALES LIBRARIES WORLDWIDE

Carl Henry
704-847-7390
www.carlhenry.com

Hi Nancy
I hope you are doing well. Wanted to help you build your sales and customer service library.

Carl

Contents

	Acknowledgements	*i*
	Introduction	*iii*
Chapter 1:	The Value of a Customer Service System	1
Chapter 2:	Internal and External Customers	13
Chapter 3:	Prepare for your Internal and External Customer	21
Chapter 4:	Engage your Internal and External Customer	33
Chapter 5:	Organize your Customer's Needs	51
Chapter 6:	Perform Quality Service	65
Chapter 7:	Leverage your Internal and External Customers' Goodwill	77
Chapter 8:	Exceed Customer's Expectations	87
Chapter 9:	Putting the People System to Work	97
Chapter 10:	People for Managers	109
Bonus:	Breaking Down Walls	119
Appendix:	Customer Care Self Survey	129

Acknowledgements

Customer service is an ever-evolving field. My clients are being asked to do more with less, and all at a time when their buyers have become more informed and discriminating than ever. So when I sat down to update this book, I did it with the knowledge that I had need to draw on the experiences of friends and colleagues who work on the front line every day.

With that in mind, I would like to pass my sincerest thanks to everyone who has helped me – directly and indirectly – over the years. By working with me in my seminars and training, and especially through your invaluable feedback, you've helped me to see and understand what works in the real world, and what doesn't. For that, I'm more grateful than you could imagine, and I hope you'll find that my ideas and solutions are as valuable to you as your continued support has been to me.

> ***If you are not happy*** *in your job, the customer **won't be happy** with your work.*

INTRODUCTION

One day, early in my professional career, I happened to stop by a small café out in the country. As I looked over the menu, I peered out the window and up into the darkening sky. Large, puffy clouds were brewing on the horizon, and I wondered if I wouldn't be better off skipping the meal and getting back on the road. I had a long drive ahead, and stormy conditions would only make things slower.

With that thought weighing on my mind, I turned to the closest patron, an older man reading the local paper, and asked him if he'd noticed the forecast. He replied that he had, and that the news had called for rain. Still, he added, a downpour seemed unlikely. He went on to explain that the Canadian winds that had built up the storm were carrying it in an easterly direction – away from my destination. He also added that the jet stream wasn't really conducive to big storms at the moment, anyway, so there probably wasn't much to worry about. The clouds looked troubling, but they weren't really cause for alarm.

Having expected nothing more than a quick answer on whether or not to expect rain, I was a bit taken aback. I was also a bit curious about where this deep well of knowledge was coming from. Was this man some kind of off-duty meteorologist?

When I asked, he just chuckled to himself a bit. As it turned out, he wasn't a weatherman at all – he was a farmer. We struck up a conversation while I drank my coffee, and he explained his fascination with the sky. Besides being interesting, he explained, weather was a mainstay of his business. Planting crops was hard work. Once they were in the ground, he couldn't afford to simply leave them to chance. During sunny stretches, he had to make sure they got water. After heavy storms, he needed to be sure none were uprooted or in need of repair. Only by constantly tending to his fields all spring and summer could he harvest them in the fall.

I think back to that impromptu meteorology lesson from time to time, especially when I'm about to give a seminar on customer service. You see, for most of my career, I've concentrated on sales – helping salespeople to improve their techniques, reach more people, and ultimately generate more orders. So why go through all the trouble of coming up with a customer service program and going on the road to teach it? Because I realized that companies work too hard planting their crops to see them blown away by a strong breeze and a bit of rain.

No matter who you work for, or where your company gets

its business, your customers are the most important asset you have. Without them, there is nothing – no departments, no products, no seminars, and no paychecks. No customers means no harvest. With that in mind, it's critical that we take the best care of them that we can.

And really, that's what this book is all about – getting better at taking care of the customers who buy our products and pay our salaries. In most cases, the advice is simple and straightforward. In fact, you may have heard a lot of my tips before. What makes *The PEOPLE System* different isn't the material; it's the way the material is used. Instead of talking about providing good service – strong, but vague advice – we'll look at specific ways to foster it. Rather than just mentioning a technique, we'll add in the *how, when,* and *why* that make the difference between a win-win with your clients and a shared headache.

As we go through the steps of the system, I want you to keep in mind just how important those customers are to your business. More than that, I want you to remember that in the customer's mind you *are* the company. That is, every interaction, no matter how short or long, you have with a customer creates an impression that extends beyond your desk or phone. In fact, for most customers, the net of those dozens of phone calls, meetings, and other interactions creates a picture that's stronger and clearer than all the logos and advertisements in the world.

So, as we make our way through the chapters and steps of The PEOPLE System, remember that in the end it all falls to you. Only you can decide how you will treat your customers, what kind of experience they'll have, and ultimately, how well you and your organization will do.

The seeds are already in the ground. It's up to you to decide how much time and energy you'll put into letting them grow. Throughout the rest of this book, you'll find a number of ways that you can help your customers – and yourself – to reap a great harvest. Let's get started…

> ***Become a**
> *hassle-free*
> *customer service provider.*

CHAPTER ONE

THE VALUE OF A CUSTOMER SERVICE SYSTEM

Every once in a while, you come across a tool that makes a task so much easier that you wonder how you ever got along without it. Take, for example, the basket. One summer afternoon, when my son was still very young, my wife and I decided to head out to the country to pick apples in upstate New York. We strolled from tree to tree, grabbing the ones that seemed the reddest and juiciest, until we had filled our container. It would have been easier to just go to a supermarket, but it was a great way to spend some time with our son and enjoy the nice weather.

The whole thing was such a hit that we decided to try it again the next year. When we arrived at the orchard, however, it became obvious that we weren't the only ones who had come up with this idea. In fact, there was a quite a crowd, by orchard standards. Dozens of families, presumably taking a break from city life, were crowded around most of the trees, and the biggest apples had already been picked. Even worse, all of the baskets were taken. But rather than come back another day, I decided that I would gather a few in my arms. After all, we had come all that way. And besides, how much difference could a basket really make?

Holding the apples I picked was easy – until I had more than two. From there, it became a frustrating endeavor. I tried cradling my arms, holding one with my chin, and even using my shirt as a makeshift holder. This last method seemed to do the trick for a while, so I piled a dozen or so on top of my stomach, and we headed for the car.

The short walk from the farmer's stand to the parking lot began to show me what a bad idea this had been. Bouncing around with each step, a few of my apples tumbled to the ground. Picking them up again was nearly impossible; each time I bent down, more fell from the pile. And once I had gathered most of them, my arms were tired and shaking so hard that I feared I might spill more. On top of that, I wasn't sure how long my tee shirt, already straining from the weight, would hold before it ripped and I lost them all completely.

To make a long story short, I dropped most of them several more times before they reached our kitchen table. I lost more than half of those apples – the same ones I had driven an hour to pick in the hot sun – and those I had left were smashed, bruised, and covered with dirt. What should have been a great experience turned out to be an enormous hassle, all because I was missing the one thing that would have made the job easy.

This would all just be a story about my habit of missing the obvious if it weren't for one thing – nearly every company

I work with is trying to handle their customers without a basket. Put another way, they're doing everything they can to fit in more buyers with advertising, marketing, and sales efforts. But once they have those customers, they aren't taking very good care of them. Many of the customers are being lost in the shuffle, and those that make it through come out on the other side bruised and scuffed. More often than not, management's answer is to spend money on CRM software or sophisticated contact-tracking schemes. These tools have their place, but what's usually needed isn't something technical or expensive. What they need is a system – a basket that keeps their customers happy and safe from spills.

That's where The PEOPLE Approach to Customer Service comes in. It takes all of the things you need to do to keep your customers happy, and arranges them into a structured plan of attack. Instead of wondering if you or your company are doing all you can for the people who keep you in business, the system keeps you on track. In other words, it takes the guesswork out of your most important tasks.

So who is The PEOPLE System for? It's for salespeople who want to take care of their customers. It's also for receptionists, who work with callers and visitors. It's for doctors who want to see their patients get the best. It's for accountants and lawyers, who want to see their clients satisfied. And, of course, it's for customer service personnel who deal with the public on the front line every day.

The point is we all have people with whom we interact.

Sometimes they're the people who buy our products. Other times, they're the people who work *with* the people who buy from us. What we call them isn't important. No matter what industry you work in, or your position within it, you have people who pay your salary. They might do it directly or indirectly, from inside or outside your own walls. This book is about giving them a higher level of service, while making things easier in the process.

Why The PEOPLE System Works

Since I first developed The PEOPLE Approach to Customer Service more than a decade ago, I've had the opportunity to share it with hundreds of companies around the world. And in nearly every case, they've reported that it's been a tremendous asset, raising loyalty amongst their customers and morale for their employees. Managers love it because it boosts profits and productivity, while their staff love the way it makes their lives easier. After a while, I started to wonder – just what makes it work so well? In doing follow-up with organizations in many different industries, I think I've figured it out. The system works because it's *simple*, and because it's *focused*.

Suppose you want to make a pitcher of lemonade. Which way would be easier, finding a recipe, or having someone go to a supermarket to read the contents of a lemonade packet to you? Most of us would rather just grab a couple of lemons and some sugar than go looking for obscure color dyes and fructose mixtures. And yet the approach that many "experts" take to customer service isn't that far off. They dig up complicated processes and procedures for each call and email, looking for the optimal way to respond to any request. Why do they do this? In my experience, it's far easier to teach people to exceed their customers' expectations, and then let them do it. I would rather do easy than hard, and so would most people I know. And if I were to explain PEOPLE's success in a nutshell, that would be it.

You see, while I would love to be heralded as a visionary, the truth is that there just isn't that much that's new or groundbreaking in my methods. In fact, there have been other people who have studied customer satisfaction and come to the same conclusions. What makes PEOPLE different isn't its techniques, it's the structure. I learned long ago that by breaking down the interactions companies have with consumers – which are by nature bound to be complicated and unique – into simple steps, you don't just make things easier, you make them *better*. Put another way, most of us want to do great work; we just need a blueprint of how to do it. The more we can make that blueprint look like a recipe for lemonade – and less like something out of a physics textbook – the more fun and effective it will be for everyone.

As I mentioned earlier, the other reason PEOPLE has held up so well has to do with its focus. Everything about it, from the acronym on down, serves as a constant reminder that *people* – that is, the internal and external customers that make our organizations "go" – should be at the center of the decisions we make. The whole thing is geared toward giving them what they need, and then a little more.

This might sound like a small point, but it's not. In today's ultra-competitive environment, it's easy to lose our perspective. We're all asked to work longer and harder than we have before. If globalization has brought one constant theme, it's "do more with less." But with all of that hustle and bustle, we can never lose sight of our customers. We need them now more than ever, and PEOPLE is designed to constantly remind us of that fact.

An Overview of The PEOPLE System

The PEOPLE System is made up of six steps, which complete the acronym and guide you through every interaction with a customer, from the first moment to a successful completion. We'll be spending the rest of this book looking at the steps and their use, but here's a brief overview:

1. Prepare for Your Customer
2. Engage the Customer
3. Organize the Customer's Needs
4. Perform Quality Service
5. Leverage Customer's Goodwill
6. Exceed Customer's Expectations

As you can see, none of these steps is overly complicated or technical. You won't have to use spreadsheets or learn a foreign language to make them work. All that's required is a brief understanding of each one, which I'm about to give you, and a willingness to try them out.

Within each step, you'll find three action guides, designed to aid you in putting the system to work. These are the essence of The PEOPLE Approach. While the acronym should help remind you of the basic ideas and focus of the program, the action guides point out what you actually need to do along the way. If you've seen me speak, then you probably received a pocket card with the steps and action guides printed on them. But if you haven't attended one of my seminars, or if you've lost your card, simply contact me at chenry@carlhenry.com, and I'll make sure you get a copy. Either way, I hope you'll keep a copy near. They aren't just the backbone of my presentation – they're a way to make your life a lot easier.

The Value of a Customer Service System

In most industries, it costs five to ten times more to bring in a new customer than it does to keep one you already have. Those are daunting numbers for any business. With that in mind, it's critical that you keep as many of your existing clients as you can. The easiest way to do that? Exceed their expectations at every turn.

It might sound obvious, but nobody ever lost a client because they were too happy, or too satisfied. As a matter of fact, not only will impressed customers stay with you, they'll often serve as magnets, drawing in new business with their praise and referrals. Working hard at customer service doesn't just help the customer – it boosts your own bottom line.

That being said, let's take a moment to look at how this translates to a personal level. After all, we all know how important customer service is to the survival and success of an organization. But beneath all the facts, figures, and positive thinking, there is another truth: *customer service is demanding.*

Today's consumers have been conditioned to fight. They've learned that their problems and questions are more likely to be met with apathy and disinterest than genuine concern or solutions. On the other side of things, departments are trying to accomplish more with less. Bigger enterprises are being supported with smaller staffs and smaller budgets. The squeeze is being felt everywhere, with customers lashing out at front-line employees, many of whom have no formal customer service training.

There's good news, though. Declining customer service standards have created a window of opportunity for those companies and employees who are willing to go the extra mile. Customers will pay a premium for superior service, and employers will spend more to keep those workers who hold up their brand. When managers look to promote, who do you think they're more likely to choose, the person who consistently outperforms his or her peers with the firm's buyers, or the one who doesn't? Which one is more likely to keep their job if the company is forced to cut back?

Nobody lets go of their most valuable staff, meaning that good customer service skills can make you invaluable to your employer.

Even putting the career benefits aside, there are a lot of reasons to embrace good customer service habits. For one thing, they'll make your life a lot easier. By following the advice in this book, you'll be taking care of your customers' problems quickly and efficiently *the first time*. How often do we shoot ourselves in the foot by rushing our interactions or jumping to solutions that don't quite fit, only to spend more time and money fixing things later? You'll find that the steps of The PEOPLE System are organized to eliminate these problems. Doing things the right way doesn't take a huge effort upfront, but it will save you countless hours and dollars down the road.

But more than that, you'll learn that customer service work can be *fun*. What's the point in dragging yourself out of bed each day if you're only going to make a half-effort? Most of us recognize intuitively that we feel better when we've done our best. That's because it's easier to have a good time when we're fully engaged in our work. As we go through the steps of the system, keep that in mind. It's up to you to decide what you're going to get out of your day. Why not make the most of it?

PEOPLE Champions

The goal of The PEOPLE System is to make you into what I like to call "a PEOPLE Champion." These are the individuals everybody likes to work with – the ones who always go the extra mile. They've mastered a few simple techniques, and as a result, they're the first to be promoted and recognized. They work hard, but they're having fun doing it. And they do it all by exceeding the expectations of the internal and external customers. In the next chapter, we'll take a look at just who those customers are, and some of the surprising places we might find them.

Something to Think About

When was the last time you sent a handwritten thank you note to a customer?

Excerpted from *High Energy Sales Thoughts: 101 Positive Sales Thoughts and Ideas* by Carl Henry

> **Don't treat your** *external customer better* *than your internal customer.*

CHAPTER TWO
INTERNAL AND EXTERNAL CUSTOMERS

When I first set out to develop The PEOPLE System, I realized right away that something was missing. I couldn't quite put my finger on it – all the major steps were there, presented in a clear way. Friends and colleagues who looked or listened to my notes on the program agreed that it was a useful tool, and audiences were responding well. Still, something wasn't quite right, and it wasn't until I had presented the program a few times that I recognized where the trouble was.

I was preparing for the second half of my talk to a large corporate group. The company had gone through a great deal of change, and customer service, always a hallmark of their business, was beginning to drop off. The executive who brought me in was particularly adamant that I impress upon the staff the importance of good service. "Customers *are* our business," he told me, "make sure they understand that without them, we have nothing."

While I certainly agree with that statement – and it's a theme I'll come to again and again throughout this book – he was only half right. Customers were the business, but he was only thinking about the ones outside his own walls. This really hit home during a break. One of the attendees, a young woman who worked in the firm's engineering department, explained that everything I was saying was good and well, but how could employees be expected to provide top-notch service to customers when they were treated so poorly by their peers?

Without realizing it, she had hit upon the missing piece of my puzzle, the nagging question in the back of my mind. *Why do so many companies treat their customers so much better than they do their employees?*

The answer is simple. Most organizations, and employees, see the buying public as a source of revenue. But they see their fellow workers as a distraction. And this frame of mind carries over into each interaction they have throughout the day.

As an example, a few years ago I walked into the office of a top executive I had known for a long time. Upon my arrival, his receptionist took my name, informed my friend that I had arrived, and offered me a cup of coffee after showing me to a seat. The receptionist didn't know me, but she knew I was on a first-name basis with her boss, and probably assumed I was a big client. In any event, the whole thing was very pleasant and courteous, and I wouldn't have thought anything more about it, had I not seen what happened a few minutes later.

While I was waiting, an employee came in and asked to speak with my friend. He had a minor issue that affected the production line, and wanted to see if he could get a couple of minutes to get a quick approval for his solution. The request seemed reasonable enough, but when she heard it, the receptionist sighed loudly. Looking down at a calendar on her desk, she announced that it would be difficult to find a free point in the schedule, but that the visitor was free to wait outside in the hall, "just in case."

Obviously, this is a terrible way to treat the people who make your company go. And it would be easy to dismiss this as a case of one person taking a small ego trip, if I hadn't witnessed other scenes just like it in companies around the world. The fact is we've conditioned ourselves to know and care about the importance of customers – so long as they're outside the building, or outside the company.

In my seminars, I like to ask attendees how many customers they have. In some cases, people think a bit and try to count their company's major buyers. Other times, they come up with numbers that include branch offices, along with a few distributors. But the most common answer, by far, is "zero." That is, most of the non-sales professionals I work with believe they have no customers. My follow up question is always the same: what about the people sitting next to you? The typical response – they're not customers, they're employees.

If this kind of thinking is prevalent at your company, let me clue you in to something – you're only doing half as well as you could be. It's true that customers are the business, but you have to count both halves – the external *and* the internal.

Who are your internal and external customers? It's simple: they're the people who buy your product or service, the people who help them, and the people who help you. This includes a lot more people than you might be used to thinking of as customers, from the buyer who signs the check to the warehouse manager who keeps your products ready to ship, and everyone in between.

If you can master this one idea that you need to treat everyone associated with your work as a customer, you'll find that you'll get more done and have an easier time doing it. Customer service might be simple, but it isn't easy. On the one hand, everybody wants more from us, and they want us to do it with less. On the other hand, we all want companies to treat us better, as employers, suppliers, and partners. But what are companies? They're *us*. It's up to every person to do better.

So as you make your way through the rest of this book and the steps of The PEOPLE System, remember that in addition to the six steps, there is really one more, the all-important first step: recognizing that your customers aren't just the buyers, they're everyone who deals with you.

Suppose your company manufactures parts that go on to retail stores. Every person who buys one is a customer. So are the distributors, and the managers and employees of the stores that carry what you sell. The employees who work in the product development, marketing and shipping departments are all customers, too, as are the maintenance and security staff. No matter where you work in the company, you have customers. And if you aren't serving the end buyer, you're helping someone who is.

Without that attitude, your business is going to be in bad shape. It took someone saying the obvious to make me realize what was missing from my seminar. Don't let it go missing from your company.

Several years ago, Sales Management Magazine ran a great article, titled "The Name Means the Same." I would like to paraphrase it for you:

- *Lawyers call them clients*
- *Doctors call them patients*
- *The Army calls them soldiers*
- *Hotel operators call them guests*
- *Newspaper people call them subscribers*
- *Radio broadcasters call them listeners*
- *Television station owners call them viewers*
- *Retailers call them shoppers*
- *Educators call them students*
- *Manufacturers call them distributors*
- *Politicians call them constituents or voters*
- *Recording artists and movie stars call them fans*
- *Bankers call them depositors or borrowers*
- *Sports promoters call them ticket holders*
- *Airline, bus, & railroad executives call them passengers*
- *Employees call them co-workers.*

No matter what name you have for the people who buy your products and services, or the ones who work beside and around you everyday, they are your internal and external customers. Keep that in mind, and treat them all accordingly.

Something to Think About

> **EXCEED THE EXPECTATIONS OF ALL OF YOUR CUSTOMERS, WHETHER THEY'RE INSIDE OR OUTSIDE YOUR WALLS**

Excerpted from *52 Things Every Sales Manager Needs to Know* by Carl Henry

> *Everyday we should*
> *seek to exceed*
> *our customer's expectations.*

CHAPTER THREE

PREPARE FOR YOUR INTERNAL AND EXTERNAL CUSTOMER

Close your eyes for a moment and think about your dream vacation. Imagine that you have two weeks in which you can do whatever you want, with no budgetary restrictions. Where would you go? Would it be skiing at a Swiss chalet, touring the pyramids in Egypt, or maybe a leisurely stay in the South Pacific? Regardless of what you envision, I want you to go one step further now. Imagine that you have only a day to pack for your trip. What would you need to bring? What preparations would you need to make?

For many people, this exercise – spending a few moments mentally arranging a vacation that they're not yet ready to take – represents more planning than they'll put into their work in a given week or month. They wouldn't dream of leaving their perfect vacation to chance, but they feel comfortable showing up to work and "winging it," day in and day out.

Sadly, they're in the majority. In this age of shoddy work, lack of attention, and a culture of excuses, most people simply don't care enough about what they're doing to think ahead. But rather than see this as an excuse to let their own performance drop off, PEOPLE Champions recognize this situation for what it is: a chance to stand out above the rest by going the extra mile.

The first step in that direction is being prepared. By attuning your mind and work environment toward success, you create the conditions to consistently shine. This shouldn't come as a surprise. The most successful people in any industry anywhere in the world are almost always those who have put themselves in a position to do well. In other words, they're always ready; they don't leave things to chance. They realize, as the old expression goes, that "an ounce of prevention is worth a pound of cure."

In this chapter we'll look at ways that you can prepare yourself for excellent customer service. As you'll see, being ready isn't that difficult, it just takes a conscious effort. Remember, the steps of The PEOPLE Approach to Customer Service are arranged to make things as easy and efficient as possible, while ensuring that you cover all the bases along the way. Toward that end, I've included three action guides for each step. These reminders are designed to lead you through the process.

The three action guides for the Prepare step are:
1. Initiate a Champion Attitude
2. Prepare Your Environment for Performance
3. Turn on Listening and Vocal Skills.

Initiate a Champion Attitude

Becoming a PEOPLE Champion starts before you ever talk to anyone. That's because your success or failure in dealing with customers is going to be determined in large part by your attitude. If you wake up ready to attack the day, eager to take on new challenges and give your very best in everything you do, it's going to be very difficult to blend in with the crowd. On the other hand, if you drag yourself out of bed feeling like you're off to a job you can't stand, determined to do the minimum necessary to get by, it's going to be really hard to get ahead, or even to have any fun, for that matter.

Of course, any number of things can affect your mood, so how can you be sure you're bringing the right attitude to work every day? The first step is simply to make a decision. Have you ever noticed how, when you expect to have a good time, you usually do? And the converse is also true. When you expect to be miserable, you almost always end up that way. With that in mind, cultivate a good attitude. Put up reminders to think positively, listen to a few minutes of upbeat music, or look over a few comic strips each morning. These little gestures can go a long way toward setting your tone for the day, and the simple act of deciding to be in a good mood will often do the trick.

Once you reach your workplace, try to clear your mind and eliminate distractions. That is, leave behind whatever you were thinking about at home, good or bad. Forget about how your favorite team won last night, or how some rude person cut you off in traffic. Simply focus on the here and now. It's tough to be positive or effective when your mind is being pulled in several different directions.

In fact, that one piece of advice – concentrate on what you're doing – is well worth the price of this book. You've probably heard that you should "focus" or "be in the moment" dozens of times, but the simple fact is that very few things can do as much for your productivity as paying attention. In our culture, it's not unusual for people to be doing half a dozen things at once. Not only that, but they're proud of it. Popular movies and television commercials reinforce the ideal of busy men and women lunching with friends while orchestrating megadeals on their cell phones and PDAs. Despite these images, however, the real world works differently. Most of us see our performance suffer from even the most minor distractions, causing us to work at a slower rate than if we handled just one thing at a time. Do whatever you're doing at the moment, and then do something else later.

It's a good idea to keep up on your industry. No matter what field you work in, there are trade magazines, seminars, and even websites that can help you stay on top of things. You don't have to spend hours a day on this, but increasing your base of knowledge can help you in a myriad of ways. Right off the bat, knowing what's happening within your company, and among your closest suppliers and competitors, gives you an edge with your customers. When they mention what's going on, you'll be able to keep up your end of the conversation and contribute valuable details. And on a more opportunistic level, it keeps you abreast of opportunities for promotions. Knowing that a key player is set to exit your organization, or that another big firm is releasing a new product, can help you spot trends before other employees see them coming. Again, you don't have to go crazy; just put in a few minutes a day to find out what's happening in your field, and how it could effect your job.

Another part of being a PEOPLE Champion is having integrity. It's important that people know they can count on the things you do and say, completely and consistently. It's not enough to *usually* do the right thing – there is no such thing as "mostly honest." Customers will forgive a lot of things, but a breach of their confidentiality is not one of them.

With that in mind, it goes without saying that you should always tell the truth and do the things you say you'll do. Beyond that, make it easy for customers to trust you. Use language that encourages them to have faith in your honesty. Don't use statements like, "I'll try," or "I think." Let them know exactly what you can and will do for them, without being vague.

A lot of this comes down to having a bit of pride in what you do. Let others know how you feel about your work, and the work of your organization as a whole. Remember, to the people you come in contact with, you *are* the company.

Most customers or employees won't have the opportunity to meet the CEO or Board of Directors. *Your* attitude and reputation are *their* attitude and reputation. That makes you more important to the customer than the so-called "important" people in your company. It's all up to you; will you be focused on helping, or on getting through your day?

There's a delivery company with which I do a lot of business. In fact, I send or receive packages with them a few times a week. Because of my route and scheduling, I mainly see two different drivers. Their respective approaches and attitudes speak volumes about how they see themselves, their company, and their chosen profession. The first is very polite. He always comes to my door with a smile, inspects the packages, and is already prepared for me to sign for any deliveries. More than that, he seems to take a real interest in what he's doing, how well he can do it, and whether the people who come in contact with him are happy.

The second driver is, shall we say, less professional. His uniform looks like it doesn't get washed frequently enough, he often leaves boxes on my driveway, and he usually seems as if I'm interrupting his nap. Not long ago, I actually saw him kick a couple of boxes out the back of his truck. Obviously, there are two very different attitudes on display here. One is trying, and the other is not. Which one do you think the company will keep if business gets tough? Which is more likely to get promoted? For that matter, which one would you rather be? Remember, both drivers have the exact same job. The only difference is that one of them has decided to make the most of it.

When you get out of bed, you have a choice to make. What's your attitude going to be? Are you going to be a PEOPLE Champion who is happy to see business coming into the company, or are you going to be down? So much of your day, your career, and your life are about deciding to have a good time and help people. Remember that, and strive to make the right choice.

Prepare Your Environment for Performance

While there's nothing as important to your success as having the right attitude, preparing your work area is critical as well. Good intentions won't make any difference without the proper tools.

No matter what your position is, or how you interact with your internal and external customers, make sure that you have equipped yourself with the basic materials or supplies you'll need. For instance, I had just checked into a hotel in Detroit not long ago and discovered I needed to break a twenty dollar bill. Strolling back to the counter, I found the employee who had taken my information, and asked if she'd be able to make change for me. After looking at me a bit absentmindedly for a moment, she replied that she'd just started her shift and didn't have any change in her drawer. If I wanted to wait a few minutes, she added, she could go and get her cash register set up.

My question is this: why hadn't she begun her shift ready to work? It seems unlikely, working the front desk cash register in a busy hotel, that she wasn't going to need change at some point. My request shouldn't have been that surprising. Obviously, she hadn't thought through the basics of what she'd need for her customers.

I wish I could say the example was unusual, but I could probably come up with hundreds of similar tales, as could most of my readers. For instance, a couple of weeks back, I tried to leave a message with a client's receptionist, but had to wait while she struggled to find a pen. On another occasion, a repairman came to my office without a screwdriver. In both cases, the tools in question – a pen and a screwdriver – are things they use dozens of times a day. Not to have either one on hand isn't just inconvenient – it's thoughtless and inefficient.

When you arrive at work, take a moment or two to think about your coming day and the tools you'll need to make it a success. What are the most important, fundamental supplies you're likely to need to do your job effectively? Do you have enough of them around, in good working order, to be sure that you won't run out?

When you're compiling this mental inventory, don't stop with just making sure you have things; also consider each item's condition. Is your computer running very slowly, or are you using a phone that cuts out? If either piece of equipment is important to your job, then dealing with those sorts of problems is bound to be an ongoing source of irritation for you and your customers.

Along those same lines, try to go beyond the obvious. Gather anything that's likely to save you time or make life easier for the people with whom you deal. Service schedules, product manuals, key phone numbers, and information from your company's website are just a few examples of tools that might make things easier and more efficient; none of them should be hard to find. In this age of instant information, there's no excuse for not having things at hand.

Turn on Listening and Vocal Skills

Customer service, at its essence, is about giving people what they want. On the surface, this seems pretty simple. And yet, many would-be PEOPLE Champions miss out on the opportunity, not because they're unwilling, but because they don't understand what their customers want.

How do we find out what our customers want? It's simple – they tell us. Most people, however, are poor listeners. Studies show time and again that the majority of us, rather than pay close attention, wait for our own turn to speak, or we let our minds drift off. But if you're going to exceed the expectations of your customers, you can't afford to miss what's being said. So how do we become better listeners? There are whole books and seminars devoted to the topic, but most of them boil it down to a couple of things: becoming a strong listener is all about being present and paying attention.

Seems simple enough, doesn't it? The fact is, though, that even when we try to concentrate, it's very easy to become distracted. With that in mind, the first step to effective listening is to prepare yourself and your workspace. You want to minimize the distractions, reducing the chance that they'll pull you away. If you have a phone, turn it off.

Televisions and radios should be silenced and put out of sight, and so should PDAs, e-mail alerts, newspapers, web pages, or anything else that will tempt your attention to stray while your customer is talking.

When you're actually with customers, ask questions and focus on what they're saying. Fight the temptation to drift off or assume that they're going to tell you something you already know. Your customers are going to tell you exactly what they want or need, and the more of it you take in, the easier your job is going to become.

In fact, it's important that you don't just listen well, but also that you *show* your customers you're listening. As they speak, give them feedback on what they're saying. Don't overdo it, but a simple "um-hmm," "ok," or "I see" once in a while will go a long way in letting them know that you're keyed in to what they're talking about.

I should point out that these rules don't just apply to listening in person. If you're dealing with your customer on the phone, you're going to have to work harder to keep yourself from being distracted. Do yourself a favor and put away your computer, unless you need it to work with your client. And you should take extra care with magazines, televisions, and anything else that could pull your focus away. Even though they can't see you, it's even more important that you show them you're paying attention. We've all had the experience of talking to a friend or colleague and realizing that they're concentrating on something else on the other end. It's not exactly flattering, and your customers won't appreciate it.

If you've done a good job of listening, then chances are your customers will return the favor. But if you want to make it easy for them, you're going to have to communicate effectively. This means speaking clearly and loudly enough for them to follow. How loud do you have to be? That depends on the situation. I attended a demonstration recently where the guide attempted to tell us about the ins and outs of his production line in the middle of a busy factory. He, like most of us, obviously had been told throughout his life that it was rude to shout at others. But in his effort to be polite, he essentially gave a talk that no one heard. While you might not talk to your customers in the midst of heavy machinery, you might still have to raise your voice a bit. Traffic, office noises, and even phone static can all cause your customers to have trouble hearing you, so remember to speak up.

Being prepared really comes down to doing your best to anticipate what you're going to need, and then getting it all together. It might be the simplest step of the PEOPLE process, but it's also one of the most critical. When you're not prepared with the tools you need, it's going to be very difficult to do a great job. At the same time, you'll likely find yourself dealing with irate customers, which isn't likely to do wonders for your performance or mood. With that in mind, my best piece of advice for this step is going to be one that I give a lot: make things easy on yourself. Prepare yourself and your environment as well as you can, and your job will be that much easier.

> *A pleasing personality* is the foundation to *excellent customer service.*

CHAPTER FOUR
ENGAGE YOUR INTERNAL AND EXTERNAL CUSTOMER

I'm not much of a car buff, so I never thought much about my tires beyond making sure they weren't too bare and grumbling when I had to pay for a new set. But then, a few years ago, one of the major manufacturers changed the way I look at tires for good. Instead of talking about radials or showing me helmeted stunt drivers weaving through cones, they pointed out a simple fact: tires are the only part of your car that touches the highway. In other words, every other safety or performance feature you have can be wonderful, but tires are where the rubber meets the road, quite literally.

It would be hard for me to come up with a better analogy for the need for strong customer service, especially at the Engage step. You see, when you work with your internal and external customers, you're translating everything that your company is about through that interaction. All the great memos and corporate initiatives might be great, but you are the driving force that will either keep the organization tight and sharp, or make it struggle to stay in one lane.

In the Engage step, things start to happen. Up to this point we've looked at topics like attitude and preparation, which are so important in setting you up for success. Now it's time to talk about what to do when you actually deal with people.

The Engage step begins when you make contact with your customer. It could be when someone walks into your office or calls you on the phone. Other times, it could be as simple as a new e-mail in your inbox. For the most part, your immediate goal will be simply to turn your attention to the customer and put him or her at ease. This might not seem like that big of a move, but it's extremely important, because it allows the other steps to happen more naturally. After all, if customers realize that you're focused on them and their needs, they're very likely to be helpful and patient. But if they sense that you just want to get rid of them, you're going to have a tough time moving forward.

Here are your three action guides for the Engage step:
1. Focus on Your Customer
2. Make Your Customer Feel Comfortable
3. Quickly Synchronize Personality Styles.

Focus on Your Customer
In the last chapter we talked about how important it is to concentrate on what you do. Being tuned in to the task at hand is probably the easiest way to do every part of your job

better. But when the time comes to actually interact with your customers, it makes *all* the difference.

It's absolutely impossible to provide great customer service without paying attention. But, as we talked about in the last chapter, most of us aren't in the habit of giving others the benefit of our complete focus. Over time, this will kill your relationships with customers, as they're forced to repeat themselves or go back over details endlessly because you weren't tuned in. If you have a tendency to drift off or let your mind wander, you'll have to overcome it. Luckily, there is an easy way to do this, and it just takes a bit of time and practice.

One of the most straightforward ways to pay attention is to simply act like you are. In other words, do all of the things you would do if you were paying strict attention to what someone else was saying – lean in, get rid of any distractions, and maintain eye or ear contact. Very often, just performing these actions will attune your mind to what's actually happening. At the same time, you're developing good listening and concentration habits that will reinforce themselves over time, while showing your customers that they matter.

The value of this last point should not be overlooked. Communication is a two-way street. You can get more from your customers by simply showing them that their concerns matter to you. Treat their problems like you would your own, and they'll probably tell you exactly how to solve them. We'll go into greater detail on this point later, but for now, just realize that every problem becomes easier to solve when you have more data about it.

Here's a quick exercise to help you stay on target: try to treat every customer the same way you would someone who knows where a hidden treasure is buried. To this end, you could even put up a small note or picture of a treasure chest somewhere around your workspace where you can see it. As silly as it sounds, using that image can help you to give your full attention. For instance, if your imaginary treasure-hunter were describing the location of a stash of riches, would you be fiddling with your PDA or clicking away on your computer? Probably not. Chances are you'd be glued to every word. And best of all, even though your customers aren't that likely to tell you where any treasure is buried, paying attention to them *will* almost certainly make you richer.

Make Your Customer Feel Comfortable

If you've ever been to a therapist or seen one on television, then you know that they always have a big comfortable sofa or chair for the client. Usually, it's pushed up next to a wall which is decorated with tranquil paintings composed with soothing colors. It isn't that every therapist in the world has the same interior designer. No, they intentionally have similar offices because they understand something about people: people, when they're relaxed, will open up a lot more. It's the same reason most people choose to confide in a close friend or a relative rather than in a brief acquaintance. They need to be at home in their surroundings – and their company – before they can really express what's on their minds.

You might not have a big comfy couch to offer your internal and external customers, but you can still make this dynamic work for you. It's not that hard; a lot of the things you do to make clients comfortable at work are the same things you'd do to make a person comfortable in your home. To start with, you can greet them warmly when they call or enter your office. If you constantly answer your door with a scowl on your face, your customers are going to be put off. But if you show them that you're glad to see them and anxious to serve them, you'll find that they'll approach you in a whole different way.

Another thing you can do is make an effort to learn and remember names. Nobody likes to be a faceless stranger. By using your customer's name, you make things more personal. People like to talk to people they know, and using customer's names reduces the mental space between you. Often, my seminar attendees are astounded at just how well this works. Give it a try. You'd be surprised how much learning and using a name can open up the conversation.

Eye and ear contact are important. In most cultures, and especially in North America, maintaining good eye contact is a powerful cue that you're paying respectful attention. In other words, letting your gaze drift around the room signals to customers that you don't really care about what they have to say. By the same token, ear contact – that is, using your active listening skills and giving verbal feedback – accomplishes the same thing, both in person and over the phone. So go ahead and let the customers know you're hearing everything they're saying, especially if they can't see your face.

Realize that you're sometimes going to have to make a bigger effort than you're used to in order either to make the customer comfortable or to get to know him or her better. Often, when clients seem rude or standoffish, it's because they're shy. You might have taken a job where you interact with others from your department and the public because you like people, but lots of your customers might not feel the same way. They may just be naturally quiet, or even nervous about meeting new people. In those cases, the best thing to do is usually to allow them to open up at their own pace. Continue to be inviting and give them a chance to talk and express themselves without feeling rushed.

Also keep in mind that different cultures view things like personal space and language differently. In other words, your idea of how closely you should stand to someone or how fast you should talk might not match your customers', especially if they come from another part of the world. Usually these minor differences are easily overcome, but make an effort to put customers at ease. If you sense that your customer is hesitant to deal with you, do your best to mirror his or her physical actions. If he or she talks quickly or slowly, try to match pace. If he or she moves closer, go ahead and allow him or her to be closer, and so on.

Making customers feel comfortable from the start will go a long way toward making your dealings with them more efficient. People who are at ease will tell you what they want quickly, freely, and clearly. The converse is true as well. When people aren't comfortable they hold back. Rather than tell you what's really on their mind, they might obscure or simply withdraw key information. They may also act out in other ways. It's not unusual for a person who feels tense or intimidated to behave in a passive-aggressive manner. This type of situation is bound to make your task more difficult, because the customer might have a need that he or she is unwilling to tell you about or help you solve. With that in mind, you should do everything you can to make them feel at home with you.

Quickly Synchronize Personality Styles

There is no single recipe for a human being. While we all share the same nearly identical genetic components, our experiences and attitudes shape us differently. The fact is, we're all utterly and inimitably unique.

And yet, people in every country and industry all over the world show remarkably similar traits. By learning to identify and work with the basic personality types that we all fall into, you can engage your customers more quickly and completely. I'll warn you that learning the styles can be a difficult skill to master at first, but with time and practice, it will become second nature.

There are four major personality styles. For illustrative

purposes, I've taken them and arranged them so that each one corresponds to a simple colored dot. For instance, "steady" personalities are green dots, "socializers" are red, and so on. This is strictly to make them fun and memorable. But I would ask you to take some time to learn the colors and their tendencies well, as we'll be referring to them through the book, and they're a cornerstone of the PEOPLE system.

Also recognize that while each of us has a dominant personality style, most of us are a mix of at least two styles. For our purposes, though, it's the dominant style that's most important, because it will tell us how best to work with our customers. Let's have a look at each one:

> **Blue** – task-oriented extroverts (Dominant)
> **Red** – people-oriented extroverts (Influencing)
> **Green** – people-oriented introverts (Steady)
> **Yellow** – task-oriented introverts (Compliant).

Blue Dots (Dominant)

As you might have guessed from their designation as "dominant," blue dots are the most aggressive style. Because of their desire for power, they like to find themselves in positions of authority. CEOs, presidents, and other "corner-office" types tend to fall into this category.

There are a number of ways that you can quickly identify blue dots. For starters, they're likely to be in management or other high power, high recognition positions. They want to be seen and respected, so you're going to find them in a corner office, not working in a secluded space where they're hidden. Blue dots want to be noticed, and they'll usually dress the part, forgoing khakis and loafers for sharp suits and flashy jewelry. They're also goal-oriented, which leads us to another tell-tale sign of a blue dot: a person who asks lots of 'when' types of questions, as in "When can I have this?" or "When will it be finished?"

Their tendency to be impatient and listen selectively can make blues difficult to work with until you've gotten used to them. Additionally, some people can be intimidated by their habit of trying to dominate a conversation. Under pressure, blues may become hostile or belligerent.

The good news is that blues tend to be one of the easier styles to talk to, so long as you work with them in a way that emphasizes their personality style. In contrast to the other styles that we'll look at in a moment, they like to move quickly and decisively, without over-thinking a problem or situation. The key to working with blue dots is to give them exactly what they want. They want to be seen and respected, so you should treat them more formally than you would some of the other styles. They respond well to someone who adopts their straight-to-the-point approach. Demonstrate that you're prepared and get down to business quickly. Give quick, direct answers to their questions; let them know that you're not wasting their time. Remember that they're selective listeners. They will pay attention to the key parts of what you're saying and ignore the rest. If you go on too long in a conversation, they may become impatient and ask you to get to the point.

Blue dots will become some of your favorite customers, as long as you can remember to move things along at their pace. Impress them with a focused approach and you'll be well on the way to a quick resolution. Appear disorganized or take the conversation too far off course and you'll quickly irritate the customer.

Red Dots (Influencers)

Red dots are the party people of your customer base. Skilled socializers, they like people and want to be liked right back. That being said, reds are easy to like. Their magnetic personalities, along with their style and flair, tend to attract others. Reds' charms aren't universal, however, as their flamboyant nature tends to irritate yellow dots.

Spotting reds is pretty straightforward. Conversationally, they generally have an upbeat personality and a positive outlook. They're more interested in people than they are technical details. In appearance, they're polished and fashionable, with a wardrobe to match their high-energy style. It's not unusual to find reds in fields where they can be seen and adored, like acting or performance, not to mention sales. In any case, reds like to talk and be around others, so they tend to be easy to find.

Working with reds is easy. Getting them to like you is as simple as letting them talk, and sharing their enthusiasm for people. When they show an interest in you, open up. When presenting solutions to reds, keep things focused on positive outcomes. Remember that they usually see the glass half full, and will be put off by negative suggestions. Also, keep in mind that reds are very image-conscious. It's important to them to look good – not only to you, but to the people with whom they work. Be sure to put them in a good light with their peers and superiors.

Like blues, reds may listen selectively and fail to absorb details, even if they appear to follow what you say. Because they have a high need for approval, they will often appear to listen intently so that you'll like them, when they're actually thinking about what to say when you stop talking. Reds don't want to be buried under a lot of technical information, either. Like the blue dots, they pay less attention to details, preferring to have things handled without too much of a hassle.

Green Dots (Steady)

For green dots, slow and steady really does win the race. That's because greens thrive on predictability and stability; they dislike change, especially when it's coming at them quickly. Of all the personality styles, green dots are the most relaxed and steady, and it will show in just about every aspect of your dealings with them.

For example, a green dot might be easy to pick out because of the simple fact that they don't like to stand out. Not showy like the blues and reds, they'll usually dress more conservatively. Another way you might pick out a green is their office decorations. Since they're usually very family-oriented, they'll likely have pictures of their loved ones prominently displayed. In conversation, greens will be slow and thoughtful. They aren't big risk takers, and like to take time to hear you and be understood in return.

Green is a very common personality style, and you'll often find them in the support areas of companies and government offices. Because they shy away from risks, they tend to gravitate toward administrative and teaching positions where they can find decent pay and steady hours.

Working with greens isn't complicated, but it does take a bit of patience. They're great listeners, so return the favor. When dealing with them, be attentive. You may have to pay close attention to find out what they're thinking, as their tendency is to hear you out completely before asking follow-up questions. Listen to what they have to say, and give them time to express their thoughts and concerns. Acknowledge their words and repeat back to them. This extra effort will help them become more comfortable with you. Remember that greens aren't naturally impulsive or decisive. They become irritated when things move too quickly, and rushing them is likely to make them even more indecisive.

Yellow Dots (Compliant)

Yellow dots are your introverted analytical thinkers. Often found in fields like engineering and finance, they like intellectual challenges that come from technical problems and lots of data.

Like greens, yellows tend to be easy-going. They prefer structure and stability to impulse and big risks. They aren't as emotional as the other styles, focusing instead on what available data will tell them about likely results.

Behaviorally, yellows will adopt a careful, systematic approach to problems. Their approach to any decision will reflect this cautious mindset. Expect them to be systematic and exacting, viewing your solutions or advice as they would any other intellectual puzzle.

It's not unusual for yellows to ask for a great deal of information, especially when it comes to backing up claims about your product or service. They want every decision to be a good one, and they will only be convinced when the evidence is strong enough. Likewise, it will be nearly impossible to resolve their concerns if you try to rush them to a decision or don't present enough information.

There's no secret to winning over yellows. Simply come prepared to offer specific answers about your solutions, especially with regard to the technical details. Remember to be patient and let them work through the analytical process. As long as you're following the steps in this book and presenting them with good answers to their problems, they'll make great customers.

In case you're wondering, TTI (the personality and productivity research firm that came up with the underlying DISC descriptions) tracks the percentage of people that exhibit each personality type as their primary style. While the percentages change slightly over time and from survey to survey, the current estimates look like this:

Blue Dot	(D)	18%
Red Dot	(I)	29%
Green Dot	(S)	45%
Yellow Dot	(C)	8%

As you can see, some styles are more prevalent than others, but you're likely to run into all of them from time to time. So what should you do with this information? You can use it to your advantage by tailoring the way you deal with customers. For instance, when you determine that a caller is a blue dot, move through the steps of The PEOPLE System quickly. If yellow dot customers come into your office, give them lots of information and technical data. Let reds talk, and respect that greens will probably take more of your time. This is one of the major strengths of the system – that you can adapt it to each individual with whom you work – so take the time to master the personality styles. Learning to recognize and effectively deal with each one is a crucial step on the way to becoming a PEOPLE Champion.

Remember, the Engage step really boils down to meeting your customers, putting your focus on them, and making them comfortable. Through that process, you will build a rapport with them and pick up on their major personality traits. Even though we've broken them down into distinct parts here, the truth of the matter is that the whole step might only take a few seconds, especially if you're dealing with a customer over the phone. The point isn't that you spend an extraordinary amount of time finding out about their greatest hopes and fears, but that you get things up and running on the right foot. Doing that correctly only takes a moment, and it will make everything else we're going to talk about that much easier.

Phone Skills

Dealing with customers over the phone isn't that different from working with them in person. You'll still use the same principles – being inviting, maintaining ear contact, and so on – but that doesn't mean you can't make things easier. Here are a few tips for working on the phone:

Minimize noise. If your office has a steady hum of conversation, ringing phones, fax machines, and so on, then try to position your phone away from outside sounds. Better yet, look into a noise-canceling headset. Not only will it reduce the noise level your caller hears, but it will also free up your hands to take notes or retrieve documents.

Speak up. Many people have a tendency to be too quiet on the phone. Make sure to speak loudly and clearly enough so that the other party can hear you.

Communicate. If you need to put customers on hold or look into their accounts, let them know. Don't keep them guessing as to what you're up to, or what will happen next.

Use hold carefully. No one likes to be put on hold and left there. If you do need to have customers wait, explain the delay and let them know how long you'll be. At the same time, never say something you shouldn't just because you think the customer is on hold and can't hear you. There are entire books and web pages devoted to customer service 'slip-ups,' where an employee said something rude or profane, only to discover that the customer could still hear. Such a lapse could lose you a customer, and even your job.

Angry Customers

Working with angry customers is a bit like diffusing a bomb – the best way to deal with one is not to have to do it in the first place. For that and many other reasons, you should always try to keep your customers happy. Still, there are going to be times when you'll have to deal with customers who are upset. Often their irritation will have nothing to do with you. It might be that their product didn't work as they thought it would, or that another person failed to meet their expectations, or that they're just having a bad day. Regardless of the reason, here are some guidelines that can help you deal with irate callers and visitors:

Remember the three C's. Usually, if you can stay calm, cool, and collected, the customer will follow suit. If nothing else, staying professional will usually prevent the situation from escalating even further.

Don't take it personally. As I said, most angry customers aren't displeased with you. In fact, more often than not, they're upset with something that's completely outside your influence. Remember that, and do your best to help them without taking things personally.

Let them talk. The best medicine for an angry customer is usually their own words. Put another way, if you give most people a chance to talk, they'll feel a lot better just from having vented and explained things. To that end, let them talk about what's bothering them. Wait until they're finished, and stop talking whenever they interrupt. Sooner or later, they'll probably calm themselves down.

Don't express tension. Avoid gestures like sighing or rolling your eyes. No matter what the customer's issue is, making him or her feel ignored or belittled isn't going to make anything better.

> *When you listen* to someone they will *tell you how* to solve their problem.

CHAPTER FIVE
ORGANIZE YOUR CUSTOMER'S NEEDS

People love puzzles. There's just something in our nature that makes us enjoy taking unordered objects and putting them together in a way that makes sense. In fact, we love our mental challenges so much that we aren't satisfied with the ones we find in our day-to-day lives. Even after we've sorted out problems at work, diagnosed cars and computers at home, and analyzed any number of situations with our friends and colleagues, what's the first thing we do? We look for a new challenge in the form of video games, television mysteries, and good old fashioned jigsaws.

Don't take it as a bad thing that we're driven to distraction, though, because our problem-solving nature is great news for anybody who wants to become a PEOPLE Champion. There's no greater puzzle than dealing with other people – all with their own sets of attitudes and experiences – and working with them can be the most fun part of the job. Every internal or external customer who comes your way has some sort of need. Sometimes they'll just tell you what it is. But more often, you'll have to figure it out based on incomplete information.

In this chapter, we'll look at the easiest and most efficient way to solve these puzzles. And then we'll move ahead and see how to best work with your solution, once you have it. While the Organize step is pretty straightforward, there's a lot involved. That's because this is the point where the interaction turns. From the first contact, you've been setting things up for a smooth ride by being prepared and making it easy for customers to engage with you. Now, using one of the world's oldest and most basic techniques, you're going to draw the information you need from them. Once you've done that, everything else is downhill. So pay special attention to what's going on in each phase of this step, and then practice it until you can move through it effortlessly.

There are three action guides for the Organize step:
1. Ask Questions to Uncover the Needs and Wants of Your Customer
2. Get an Agreement That You Have Identified Your Internal and External Customers' Needs
3. Recommend Service That Will Satisfy Needs.

Ask Questions to Uncover the Needs and Wants of Your Customer

If there's one thing you could say about our culture, it's that we've become great question askers. We want to know everything, all the time, especially if we feel like information is hidden from us. So it's no surprise that the brightest in nearly every profession – be they doctors, lawyers, journalists, or detectives – cut to the heart of problems by using skillful inquiries. The end result, whether it's a stunning diagnosis or a tearful confession, might be a great dramatic moment, but it always follows from asking the right things at the right times.

As a customer service professional, you probably already know that questions are important to your success. After all, how else can you get customers to tell you about their needs? But even so, most of the groups I work with find that they have room to improve. That's because it isn't just about asking questions, it's about asking the *right* questions the *right* way.

For example, you might not realize how important it is to ask questions that are specific. With a focused inquiry, you can cut straight to the heart of the problem. But, on the other hand, if your questions are vague and unclear, you're likely to get answers that feel the same way.

Most of us understand this in a practical sense, because of the way we use questions in our day-to-day lives. For instance, you might ask a friend, "How's the weather?" if you're just interested in making small talk. You might not really care if it's sunny or raining; you just want to get a conversation rolling. If you are asking for a more specific purpose, however, your question would probably be more direct. Suppose you were planning a trip to the beach. Instead of asking about the weather in general, you might ask, "Have you heard whether it's going to rain on Saturday?"

In this case, and most others, the more specific question is the better one, because it cuts to the heart of what you really want to know.

As a general rule, most of the questions you put to customers should follow a path from the vague to the specific. You might open up a meeting or phone call with, "How may I help you today?" As the conversation moves on, though, try to make your questions more and more specific. Doing so will save you both time and help you zero in on solutions more quickly.

It's also important to know the difference between open-ended questions and closed-ended questions. Closed-ended questions, the ones people tend to ask, are those that require a "yes" or "no" response. Open-ended questions, on the other hand, invite a more expansive answer. An example of a closed-ended question might be, "Is your product working properly?" Your customer might answer that it is, or that it isn't. There's even a chance they could go on to tell you more, but you haven't asked for it. The same thing could be asked in a much more open way by saying something like, "Tell me about how your product is working today."

Can you feel the difference between the two questions? While the first question only asked whether the product is working or not, the second question asked the same thing, but also invited the customer to give more detailed feedback. In other words, it opened up the conversation by showing a bigger interest.

If the second approach seems subtle, know that its

effects aren't. I can guarantee that this approach will net you more information from your customers in a much shorter time frame. That's because open-ended questions don't just get you more by asking for longer answers, they also show the customer that you want to hear what they have to say. Customers have long been trained that dealing with any customer service professional is likely to be tedious and aggravating. They expect that you're going to give them a minimal amount of attention, along with stilted questions and boilerplate answers. It's unfortunate that they tend to think of the companies they do business with this way, but they've been conditioned to do so over the years by lazy people and understaffed, under-funded customer care departments. By asking open-ended questions, and using your listening skills, you can go a long way toward breaking down their natural resistance. And as we saw in the last chapter, comfortable people will tell you what they want and expect from you more quickly and honestly.

I should point out that this is the place in the PEOPLE process where your customer's personality style will make the biggest difference. Blue dots, fast and impulsive by nature, may try to rush through your questions and their answers. You may be tempted to let them hurry, but don't allow things to go so quickly that you miss out on important details. Red dots, on the other hand, like people; so, they may engage you with questions about yourself, or want to talk about the interpersonal nature of their situation. These are both fine, so long as you keep things focused on how you can help them. Green and yellow dots, for the most part, are the biggest challenge, because they will sometimes need a bit of extra prodding. Naturally reserved, they may take extra time to get comfortable with you before disclosing their real concerns. The best thing to do is just draw them out as well as you can, paying special attention to the types of questions you ask.

By making a conscious effort, you'll probably get into the habit of asking good, focused, open-ended questions in just a couple of weeks. But don't stop there. As great a tool as good questions are, they're most effective when used in tandem. In other words, there's no one or two magic things you can ask that will tell you all you need to know. The key is to use follow-up questions effectively. Ask something, get an answer, and then ask something else that moves you closer to a definitive picture of the client's situation. When should you stop? When you feel absolutely sure you know what the customer's problem is. Give up before that point, and you risk working with incomplete information. You might get away with it once in a while, but it's usually just going to mean more time and effort in the long run.

As one final point on asking good questions, it's wise to take good notes. They don't necessarily have to be detailed, but you never know how jotting down a few words as your client is speaking will help you. For one thing, it's likely to help you concentrate on the conversation. Your mind is much less likely to drift if you're following your customer's words with a pen. In a more practical sense, your notes might yield follow up questions that you want to ask after the customer has finished speaking. Putting them down in the margin will ensure that you won't forget. It will also give you a chance to keep the pertinent information in front of you without dividing your attention. If you need to refer back to something that was said, like a product number or client names, you can do so without making them repeat themselves.

I hope I've driven home the message that asking great questions is the first step to getting great answers. Learning which ones to ask and the right way to do it will provide you with a great skill. It won't just make you faster and more efficient; it will also make you more fun to be around. Everybody loves a great listener – just ask them.

Get an Agreement That You Have Identified Your Internal and External Customers' Needs

Getting an agreement that you have identified your customers' needs, or taking a moment to tell them what you've heard from them, is one of the most frequently skipped steps of any customer service system. And yet it's one that you can't afford to gloss over.

You'd think that, with all of those questions and notes, we would be able to just identify the customer's needs and move on to a solution. Unfortunately, this is usually a bad idea. There are a few reasons, but the biggest one is that we sometimes get things wrong.

But how could we miss out, with all of that information being gathered? Because even though we might be listening, we don't always hear what's being said. Just as it's human nature to seek out puzzles, it's in our DNA to find patterns and solutions as well. In other words, your mind gets to be very good at filling in gaps, especially in situations where it's used to seeing the same results again and again. Think of the way children, after finishing their first few jigsaw puzzles, can finish them more quickly, or how you can finish a familiar ad after hearing only a second or two. When you get used to something, it gets easy to jump ahead.

When it comes to customer service, this tendency can become problematic. Each caller or visitor has a problem that is unique in their own minds, but you're likely to have heard of something like it many times before. So, as they begin describing their situation, it's only natural that you want to move on to the solution. Skipping through the tedious details seems like a great way to save time, not to mention to fight off boredom.

But, as I mentioned before, situations, even those that look similar, are often unique. What looks like a cold turns out to be the flu, and vice versa. What I'm saying is that you can't make assumptions. Even if you're ninety-nine percent sure what your customer needs, let him or her tell you about their situation anyway. There's always the chance things won't turn out to be the way you expected, and by working through the steps you can ensure you won't have to backtrack needlessly.

Besides, if we jump ahead too quickly, our solutions aren't likely to be welcomed anyway. Customers only listen to us after we've listened to them. They won't pay attention if they feel we've rushed them. With that in mind, it's very important to ask the right questions to find out their needs, and then show them that you've heard them. You don't need to make a long elaborate speech; simply reiterate what they've told you they need or would like. In most cases, they'll simply agree that you've summarized their situation and appreciate your attention. But once in a while, this step will stop you from compounding a misunderstanding. For instance, the customer might point out an aspect of the problem that he or she forgot to mention, or correct something that you misheard. In either case, offering this short pause will save you a lot of time and effort down the road, either by gaining the customer's trust, or by fixing a mistake before it's carried on to the next step.

Recommend Service That Will Satisfy Needs

Once you've identified your internal or external customers' needs, and gotten their agreement that you understand them, you'll make suggestions to remedy their situations. Because the individual solutions you come up with will depend on your industry, the customer, the problem at hand, and so on, I'm not going to recommend anything specific. Besides, most of your company's solutions probably are covered in your training, manuals, or by advice from a supervisor. So, with that in mind, let me give you some general points to consider.

First, never tell customers what to do. Ask questions and recommend possible solutions. Since you've demonstrated that you are a professional qualified to help, your opinion should carry a lot of weight.

It's also a good idea to put the customers first. You want to think about their problems, and your solutions, in terms of what they need, not what you'd like. The only thing that matters to them is having their problems fixed as quickly and easily as possible. They don't care what takes the least amount of time for you, or what will be the least amount of hassle. They shouldn't – that's our job. Do what you can to make things as simple as possible for them, and you'll be doing the best for yourself in the long run.

When you're presenting solutions, try to frame them in a conversational tone. Few things are as boring as a heavy dose of technical language, jargon, obscure acronyms, or heavy industry-speak. Those kinds of things don't just turn customers off; they make them think you're trying to hide something from them, even if you aren't.

Whenever possible, use 'we' language. Sometimes, just using that word can pull a customer into agreement. Subconsciously, it positions the two of you together, against the problem, instead of against one another. For example, when recommending an action, say, "I think *we* should…" instead of, "I think *you* should…." Customers will notice the difference, and you'll have an easier time leading them to the best solution.

Expect that your customers are going to want their problems to be solved urgently. They're committed to getting answers right now, and they're going to expect the same from you. Let them know that their time frame is important to you, and that you'll do whatever you can to help them find an immediate answer.

And no matter what, never give the customer incorrect information or offer up excuses. "I've been on vacation," "you didn't use it correctly," or "I can't help you with that" are never satisfactory answers to people's problems. Remember, the biggest part of being a PEOPLE Champion is attitude. Keep your focus where it belongs – on helping your internal and external customers – and let it show in the way you treat them.

Don't be surprised if your blue and red dot customers take your advice right away. They like quick solutions and aren't likely to agonize over decisions. Green dots, however, may ask you about your solution in different terms, like costs, time frames, and so on. It's not uncommon for yellow dots to ask to see more written information, especially in terms of technical details and case studies. Be patient and arm them with as much data as possible; they like to be sure they're making the right call before they commit to anything.

With the Organize step, we've gotten to the heart of what makes great customer service – asking good questions, paying attention to the answers, and recommending the right solutions. When customers come to you it's because they have a problem or situation that they haven't been able to solve on their own. They're looking to you for answers, but you're never going to be able to give them those answers if you can't find out what their situation is from the beginning.

So take advantage of your good listening skills by letting them talk. Customers love to hear their own voices. And the more they say, the easier things are going to be for you.

Sample Questions

Great customer service is all about asking the right questions. With that in mind, here are a few to get you started:

- What services do you think you may need in the future?
- What can I do to exceed your expectations?
- How much time do I have to solve your problem?
- How often does this problem occur?
- When was the last time you modified that procedure?
- Who else will be involved in the decision?
- What changes would you like to see?
- What has and has not worked in the past?
- How do you think you could better use my services?
- How satisfied are you with the response time you received?
- How do you think the problem developed?
- Why did you decide to take that action?
- What else can I do to satisfy your needs?
- What did someone else do to exceed your expectations?
- What should I have done to appropriately follow up?
- Where do we stand concerning the problem?
- What is the specific nature of the problem?
- What do you hope to accomplish today?
- What other services may I offer?

Of course, it's up to you to figure out what questions are appropriate for your customers in your business. But I hope that these examples will get you started on the right track.

> **Don't promise** *something you know you can't or won't deliver.*

CHAPTER SIX
PERFORM QUALITY SERVICE

A number of years ago, I was returning home from giving a seminar on The PEOPLE System, and I found myself sitting in an airport waiting for my flight to board. This isn't an unusual situation for me, and I'll usually just open a book or catch up on a bit of work. On this particular day, however, the Olympic Games were in full swing, and some of the public monitors were showing highlights.

As images of sprinters, gymnasts, and other spectacularly gifted individuals floated by, I was struck by the commentary that accompanied them. One after another, the announcers praised the athletes for having *"performed* on the world's greatest stage." That word, which I had included in my program years before, caught my attention, because I had never really considered in how many ways it gets used. In some cases, like with those sportscasters, it can mean to come up big. Other times, as with a symphony performance, it can mean a public display of art. Or it can simply mean to do something, as in "perform a simple task."

In each of these cases, however, *perform* really just means to do what you've been preparing to do. You can be sure those Olympians have gone through their motions and routines thousands of times. The symphony has rehearsed endlessly to ensure a flawless performance. And even the most basic tasks that we're asked to perform are usually preceded by some kind of training or repetition.

And really, that's what the Perform step boils down to – getting something done. Everything has been leading up to this. You've asked questions, gathered ideas, and gotten agreement from your customer. Now, all that's left is just to do whatever it was you recommended or agreed upon.

But just because this is a simple step, don't think there aren't ways to go the extra mile. Like everything else in life, you'll have a choice to either provide superior service or just do the minimum to try to get by. And as with all the other steps, you can make things a lot easier for yourself by doing the hard work up front.

Let's take a look at the three action guides for the Perform step:

1. Deliver Promised Service
2. Deliver Service as Promptly as Possible
3. Get Internal and External Customer's Feedback That He or She is Satisfied.

Deliver Promised Service

This one is simple. You have to do what you say you're going to do. Whether you promise a follow-up phone call, a brand new product, or something even bigger, you have to deliver. Don't change your mind, and don't leave anything out. Actions always speak louder than words, and people desperately want to work with others that they can trust to keep to their agreements.

As basic as that might be, it's a point that lots of professionals miss. The world is full of men and women who are convinced they have "good people skills." Because they can schmooze customers and hold up their end of a conversation, they naturally assume that customers like them and will want to work with them. While there is definitely some truth to that sentiment – being personable can do a lot for your success – there's no substitute for being reliable. In other words, nobody cares how bright, funny, or good-looking you are if you can't or won't help them with their problems. This is especially true of your internal and external customers. They have family and friends they can turn to for companionship. What they need from you is solutions.

Always keep that in mind, and don't promise anything you can't or won't do. Keeping your word and delivering what you say you will isn't just easier, it's also the best "people skill" you can have.

Deliver Service as Promptly as Possible

When it comes to pleasing your customers, there is no time like now. We live in a world of shrinking margins and looming deadlines, where "just a little later" is often the same as "way too late." Yes, it's unfortunate that people want everything yesterday. But remember, they're facing similar demands from their internal and external customers. Their jobs might depend on you getting things done on time. And in a certain sense, yours probably does, too.

To look at this another way, consider a survey conducted by McGraw-Hill. In looking at consumer satisfaction in various industries, they came upon an interesting piece of information: once wait times go over five minutes, customer service satisfaction drops dramatically. That is, when customers were kept waiting in lobbies, on the phone, or elsewhere, they reported that they were far less satisfied with their service, *regardless of what happened after that point.* The same applies to your follow-up. The longer your customers have to wait for you to do what you say you're going to do, the less happy they're going to be about it.

So what does this mean to you? It goes without saying that you should do your best to get to people right away. Try not to leave them waiting, regardless of whether they've contacted you in person, on the phone, or through e-mail. And if you must delay, because you're finishing up with another customer or are overwhelmed at the moment, at least acknowledge them and let them know you'll be with them shortly.

Beyond that, once you've attended to your customers, put your solutions into place for them as promptly as possible. It's amazing, among professionals with lazy habits, to see how quickly the wind falls out of their sails once the customer is no longer right in front of them. What once seemed urgent

– the return phone call, the new product part, the e-mail to the service department – suddenly finds itself in the "to do later" pile.

Don't fall into this trap. If the remedy is something that you can take care of, or at least get started right away, then do so. And if an immediate solution isn't possible, let the customer know what he or she should expect next – and when – and then do everything you can to meet or beat that deadline.

Never promise anything you can't deliver, though. This will rankle all of your customers, but especially your blue and red dots, who want things done yesterday, if not sooner. As you'll recall, the name of the game for a PEOPLE Champion is to *exceed* customer expectations, not to barely meet them or just come close. In order to do that, you're going to need to have good habits, especially when it comes to being prompt. Procrastination will kill your customer satisfaction, and eventually your career as well. So if you find yourself putting things off, check out the page at the end of this chapter. It has some great tips for getting things done right away. If you still struggle, walk into your local bookstore and check out a few titles on the topic. Procrastination is a deadly habit, and if you don't beat it now, you'll probably never come back to it later.

Get Internal and External Customer's Feedback That He or She is Satisfied

When you've done what you said you were going to

do, how do you know whether or not you've solved your customers' problems? Easy: you ask them. Getting feedback – a cornerstone of The PEOPLE System – hardly ever takes more than a minute, and it's the only way to really know whether you've done your job. So why is it that most people skip this step?

The answer, of course, is that most people *don't want* feedback. In fact, the last thing in the world they want is to give their customer a chance to ask them for something else. They're used to doing the bare minimum to get by, and they hope to solve the problem just well enough that the customer won't bother them again. With that mindset, they take a "no news is good news" approach and get their customers off the phone or out of the office as quickly as they can.

As I'm sure you've guessed by now, we're not going to do that. In The PEOPLE System, there is no easy way out. The good news, though, is that forming good habits will repay you tenfold down the road in saved time, less aggravation, and yes, more money.

That's because everything we're doing here, even though it might take more effort at first, is designed to eliminate extra work and problems later. Early on, we make the customers feel comfortable so we don't have to wrestle information out of them. Then we take the time to ask careful questions and be sure that we're correctly diagnosing their problems. And now we're going to pause and make *absolutely sure* they're satisfied, because if we don't, then we're likely to face a bigger problem down the road, or at least find ourselves doing the same work that we tried to skip before.

I point all of this out because checking to see whether your customer is satisfied is one of the easiest ways that most customer service departments and professionals can improve their performance. Often, when I present the PEOPLE seminar, I like to poll the audience. In a recent group of more than five hundred people, I found some startling numbers. Only 29% said they always checked to see if their customers were completely satisfied with the service they received, 39% usually did, 25% said they sometimes asked, and 7% admitted that they rarely or never bothered. But if they aren't asking their customers about their satisfaction, how do they really know how well they're doing? They don't. Either they guess, or they just don't care at all. They figure if no one has called and complained, things must be going great. That's not good enough; we have to be more proactive. Do you really want happier customers, or are you just pretending? This is where we'll find out.

So when you've finished with your clients, find out how happy they are (or aren't). It only takes a moment, and if you've been following the steps of the PEOPLE system so far, then you shouldn't be in for any nasty surprises. Still, things happen in the real world. It could be that you did everything in your power, but the customer still isn't happy. It might be that a replacement part showed up late, or damaged. Or perhaps another person's follow-up wasn't as prompt or strong as your own. Whatever the reason, when you find your customer *isn't* happy, take that information for what it is and make the most of it.

To the uninformed, complaints look a lot like interruptions. But to PEOPLE Champions, they're important messages. When a customer complains, they aren't just telling you what's wrong – they're giving you a chance to fix it. And those chances don't come along as often as you'd think. Consider the conclusions of a *Consumer Affairs* study. Upon surveying all kinds of buyers about why they'd taken their business from one vendor or company to another, they found that 68% – a whopping two thirds – left because they felt they were treated without care or concern by an owner, manager, or frontline employee. This is why The PEOPLE System is important.

In the same study, researchers found that of the unhappy majority, 96% never complained. However, a full 90% of them will never buy from the offending agent again, and most will tell nearly a dozen other people of their bad experience.

So treat complaints like the golden opportunities they are. You aren't going to be able to please everyone, but when you can, you often end up with customers that are more loyal than they would have been if nothing had gone wrong in the first place. Nothing shows attention like fixing an error promptly. Turning wrongs into rights makes customers into good customers, and good customers into lifetime clients and friends. What's more, businesses have been doing such a bad job of taking care of customers that making things right can set you apart as a business.

If those weren't reasons enough, remember that new customers are expensive. In most industries, it takes at least five times as much to bring in a new customer as it does to service an existing one. You don't have to do a lot of math to realize fixing problems now will likely save you a bundle later. You simply cannot afford unhappy customers. Give them the chance to tell you about their experience and satisfaction, and you're unlikely to have enduring unhappiness among your clients.

Much of this chapter could be boiled down to some simple advice: do what you say you're going to do, do it quickly, and then find out if it did the trick. Keep to those guidelines and things should go smoothly for you; and when they don't, you'll have the tools to fix things.

In the next chapter, we'll look at what to do with all those happy customers you've been building up by following this system. As you'll see, they can go from being a tough responsibility to an enormous asset.

Beating Procrastination

If you're going to become a PEOPLE Champion, or just succeed in your career, you're going to have to beat procrastination. But deciding to do things now instead of later is easier than it sounds if you're already in the habit of putting things off. Here are some tips to get you started:

Stop making excuses. Procrastination is an international phenomenon. If it was a club, we would all join it…tomorrow. For that reason, you might have a lot of friends and colleagues that procrastinate. Try to spend your time with people who get a lot accomplished. Habits rub off, and you need to surround yourself with good influences.

Keep a schedule. It's amazing how quickly days and hours disappear. If you've ever had a three-day weekend that seemed to end just as it began, then you know what I mean. Just as television, video games, and other distractions can eat away your free time, coffee breaks, the internet, and long phone calls can put you behind in the office. Set aside blocks of your day to get things done. This habit will make it easier to stay disciplined enough to ignore things that are less important.

Be prepared. Everything is easier and faster when you have things like product knowledge, working equipment, and supplies at hand. Having to hunt for things can tempt you to wait to get started, so begin your day ready to work.

Be organized. Keep a list of everything you've promised to do or deliver somewhere around the office. Having a visual reminder can keep you on task.

Keep goals in mind. It's always easier to do the hard work now if you keep in mind how much better you'll feel later when it's done. If you're having trouble getting to work, ask yourself: would I rather be finished with this, or having it still hanging over my head? The answer will usually spur you back to work.

Something to Think About

Doing a lot of things is not the secret to success.

You must do the right things.

Excerpted from *High Energy Sales Thoughts: 101 Positive Sales Thoughts and Ideas* by Carl Henry

*"**In the customer's eyes**
you are
the company."*

CHAPTER SEVEN
LEVERAGE YOUR INTERNAL AND EXTERNAL CUSTOMERS' GOODWILL

Archimedes, the Greek mathematician who made numerous discoveries in geometry, hydrostatics, and mechanics, once famously proclaimed, "Give me a lever long enough and I'll move the world." While he might have been more concerned with light topics like the expression of Pi and the summation of an infinite series of integers, his attitude applies just as well to customer service.

A lever, you see, is nothing more than a multiplication of effort. As a tool, a lever allows you to move objects that you wouldn't be able to manage with your own strength. In finance, the practice refers to buying securities and investments with a small down payment; in other words, you *leverage* a small amount of money to make a very large purchase.

So how does any of this apply to the PEOPLE system? Well, after all the hard work we're putting into making sure that our customers are as happy as they can possibly be, why not use them to get more out of our efforts? Why not leverage the goodwill we've created to get more business, not to mention promotions and other benefits? In this chapter, we'll see how you can do just that.

There are three action guides for the Leverage step:
1. If Appropriate, Offer Additional Services
2. Reinforce Customer Care Values
3. If Internal or External Customers Exhibit Extreme Satisfaction, Encourage Them to Pass on the Goodwill to Others.

If Appropriate, Offer Additional Services

Want to know the best time to get your customer to buy something from you? It's the moment when they're happy with what you've already done for them.

Having spent much of my career working in sales, this seems like a natural impulse to me. After all, who couldn't use more business? Too often, however, I see all kinds of professionals in and out of sales go to great lengths to solve a customer's problem only to say, "Thanks" and walk away. They're missing out on a golden opportunity, and I don't want you to make the same mistake.

Providing great customer service is one of the best ways to increase your bottom line (and monthly or yearly bonus). After all, when people are happy with you, aren't they likely to want to keep working with you? Take advantage of that impulse and see if you can get a new sale, or even a future commitment.

Note that you don't have to make a big deal or give a formal presentation to make something happen. More often than not, it can boil down to something as simple as telling the customer, "Thanks again for your business; I'm glad everything turned out well. In fact, I would like to make sure we can give you the same kind of service next year. Could we set up a time to talk about your next order?" Or, if you're looking to generate an add-on sale, you might try something like, "I'm glad you were pleased with the way we handled things. By the way, did you know there was an extra service plan available for that model?"

The key here is speed. Customers love it when you go the extra mile for them, but they have short memories. If you wait a week or a month before you follow up, you risk the chance they'll forget why they like you and your company so much.

Obviously, you'll have to use your common sense. If the reason your service had to be so great was that you bungled the order so badly the first time around, then you might not want to push too hard for another sale. But even if things didn't go as smoothly as they could have, your customers will probably appreciate you doing what you can to fix things promptly. The world is full of firms giving terrible customer service. Show them you can get things done, and that you'll take care of any problem, and you'll find yourself with a loyal group of customers.

Whether you're in sales or not, try to remember that it's easiest to get new orders while customers are happiest. So do anything you can to keep in their good graces, and look for more business while you're there.

Reinforce Customer Care Values

A few years ago, I went to visit one of my favorite clients up in Canada. My contact, the sales manager for a forestry equipment firm and a longtime friend, asked me to have lunch after our seminar. He mentioned that he wanted to stop and visit a customer along the way. I was in no hurry, so I agreed to the trip.

After packing up my things, I piled into his car and we set off. At first, the trip was like any other. We went from their facility onto a few city streets and eventually a highway. But as the drive wore on, we left the city behind and ventured deep into thick forests. Finally, we exited the highway and zipped our way through winding back roads, occasionally spotting deer and other wildlife between the towering pines.

After more than an hour, just when it seemed like we might be lost, my friend pulled onto a small gravel trail that led up to a group of big sheds. In each one sat a handful of massive tractors, and a middle-aged man in overalls pulled himself out from one of them to meet us.

My friend and his customer greeted each other warmly, talked for a few minutes about their families and the weather, and then walked over to the machinery. For a few minutes, my friend showed the man a couple of features that weren't explained well in the manual, and made sure he'd have no trouble using them when he left. Finally, he wrapped their interaction up by saying, "Well, I guess I just wanted to stop by and see how you were getting along. Thanks again for your business, and let me know if there's anything I can do for you."

The whole thing couldn't have taken more than ten minutes, but I knew at that moment where to find an example of a true PEOPLE Champion. How many people would have bothered to make a two or three-hour round trip journey to thank a customer – especially a small one – for his business? How many would have been satisfied to just send a card or make a phone call?

It's that rarity that makes my friend so special. He's willing to do anything he can to let his customers know he appreciates their business. As a result, they love working with him. I've never been back to that forest road, and in truth I probably couldn't find it if I wanted to, but I would be willing to bet he still has that customer, and will for as many years as he wants. I don't think that man would dream of buying from anyone else. Would you?

Reinforcing customer care values – letting people know you're happy to have their business – is a great way to generate and leverage goodwill. Simply treat every customer as if they were your favorite and most important. As an added benefit, not only will they all feel better about working with you, but chances are you'll start to feel better about them, too. It's human nature. The better you are to those around you, the better they'll be in return. That kind of back and forth creates a positive feedback cycle where your buyers become great clients, for no other reason than you treating them that way.

When you get a new account, or have the opportunity to work with someone for the first time, send a handwritten thank-you note. Hardly anyone takes the time to do that anymore, and it's a gesture that everyone can appreciate. When you have longer-term clients, reward them for continuing to do business with you. A nice lunch, a pair of tickets, or even a gift card can go a long way toward building goodwill. Spending a lot isn't important; showing your customers you appreciate their repeated business is.

If Internal or External Customers Exhibit Extreme Satisfaction, Encourage Them to Pass on the Goodwill to Others

To get the most out of the PEOPLE Customer Service System, you'll have to learn something that politicians already know: no good deed is truly great until lots of people know about it. In all seriousness, you should be doing your best for your customers because it's the right thing, and because it will make your job that much easier and profitable in the long run. Still, there's nothing wrong with getting a little extra publicity out of it if you can.

To that end, I encourage you to try to make good use of the positive feedback that your customers give you. There is a good way and a bad way to do this, and if you're shaking your head or rolling your eyes at the thought of it, then you've probably already seen the bad way.

Many "experts" in customer service and other fields will advise you to take a course of action that basically amounts to fishing for compliments. As this line of thinking goes, most of your customers, as long as they aren't too disgruntled, can probably be pestered into giving you some kind of recommendation, be it verbal, written, or otherwise. And so, they tell you, you should ask everyone who comes into contact with you if they'd be willing to endorse you as a shining example of the human race.

While that approach might work some of the time, it's not one that I recommend. For one thing, pestering customers isn't a great way to keep them as customers. And besides, what sort of kind words are you really going to get by hunting for them?

A better tactic is to follow the advice in this book, make sure that your customers are absolutely, positively, flat-out ecstatic with the service you've given them, and then *let them* tell you how happy they are. Then – and only then – do you ask them if they would pass along their comments.

For example, suppose you fix a really big problem for one of your clients. You diagnose the situation, recommend a solution, and then deliver on it promptly. When it's all over, they give you a call and thank you once more for your help, mentioning that they really appreciates all you've done. At that point, it's not a bad idea to ask if they wouldn't mind saying the same thing to your supervisor, another customer, or some other person "if the opportunity comes up."

Sometimes, despite their enthusiasm and best intentions, the customer will simply forget. But other times, they won't. And those recommendations – specific comments about how you helped with an actual problem – will be more genuine and more effective than anything you could have staged.

I've seen clients of mine use this to great effect for years. Because they provided superior service, they know that many of their customers will offer kind words. Of those, some will speak to their supervisors. Others will talk to department heads and other persons within the company. Still more will talk to other companies, or buyers within their own organizations. Over time, these comments – that leveraged goodwill – become like a force propelling their careers. It sweeps them into greater sales, bigger offices, and more responsibility. Never discount the power of a satisfied customer's words. They can travel a lot farther, and a lot faster, than you might think.

At the same time, leverage goodwill internally as well. Everyone likes to be appreciated, and yet we work in a culture where most people's work is a thankless endeavor. Showing other employees that you care can help foster teamwork, or at least make someone's day.

It's a shame that more of us don't make a conscious effort to build each other up. It's not uncommon for a supervisor or co-worker to speak up when they see something done incorrectly, but you can just as easily say something when you see someone step up and perform brilliantly. If you see someone providing really excellent service, make sure your team members get a heads-up.

This is especially important if you're a manager. In many departments, supervisors become accustomed to leading by crisis. Overwhelmed, they look for breaks in the system and do their best to clear them out. Not only does this lead to greater stress, but it encourages frontline workers to see things from an "us versus them" point of view with management. If the only feedback you pass along is negative, your team is going to pick up on that. There will always be times when you'll have to administer criticism or ask for greater effort, but balance those times with some positive messages as well. Everyone will feel better, and the individuals you supervise might just do the same thing for you.

> ***Just do a little more** than you said you were going to do, and you will have a happy customer.*

CHAPTER EIGHT
EXCEED CUSTOMERS' EXPECTATIONS

Think of the best service you've ever gotten at a restaurant, in a store, or on an airline. I'm willing to bet that no matter where it was, or who gave you the great service, it wasn't just that things went smoothly; it was that someone did that *little extra bit* to make such an impression.

I know in my own mind, next to the hundreds of customer service nightmares I've witnessed and been told about, a few instances stand out in which someone went the extra mile for me. And in most cases, I don't just remember the person who helped me out, but the company as well. Consequently, I go out of my way to do business with them as frequently as possible.

During this step, we're going to look at ways you can make the same kind of impression on your clients. More often than not, you won't have to do anything extraordinary. In fact, by simply looking for opportunities to show your customers that you're thinking of them, you're likely to find dozens of easy things you can do that will make a huge impact on their satisfaction. But even though your effort might be small, the impact will be huge, because customers won't just be happy – they'll tell you and lots of other people just how happy they are.

Here are the three action guides for the Exceed step:
1. Think Creative Extra Value
2. Execute Your Idea Quickly
3. Critique Your PEOPLE Success.

Think Creative Extra Value

What is it about what you do, or what your company provides, that gives value to your customer? Try to think beyond the obvious. While it might be true that you manufacture cars or computers, you might also be offering speed, comfort, or convenience.

I once read that George Washington Carver came up with more than three hundred different uses for the peanut. In other words, where his competitors saw a seed or a snack, he dreamed up countless other ways to derive value from his product. You can do the same kind of thing by thinking like your customers. Is there some aspect of what you offer that could be of use to them? Is there another product, or a piece of information, that would make their lives easier?

Often, the clues can be found by simply paying attention. For example, suppose you work for a company that makes machine tool parts, and your customer mentions that he or she has been using your equipment to open up more production shifts. You might forward them an article you come across on managing employees when you extend the workday. Or if you noticed that they are having trouble with a sticking gear shift, you could offer to send a technician to mend the part and explain how to reduce wear and tear.

How much time would either of those actions take you? How much of a difference would they make to your customer? Those two answers – the essence of how something small can save another person a lot of time – are what exceeding expectations is all about. It's asking yourself what more you can do, and then making it happen.

Execute Your Idea Quickly

When you find something you can do for your customer, do it quickly. As with the Perform step, remember that time can be your most valuable ally or your biggest enemy. There's an enormous difference between finding something of value for your customers and providing it when they need it and waiting around for a few weeks to get around to it. One signals that you want to be of service to them; the other says that you don't really care.

Almost every opportunity, in life and in business, comes with an expiration date. Worst of all, we rarely know exactly when it is. So if you find yourself with a chance to shine, take it before it's too late.

Critique Your PEOPLE Success

As a speaking professional, I get to meet a lot of different types of people. In my industry there are mountain climbers, plane crash survivors, hypnotists, and best-selling authors. But one of the most interesting groups, bar none, is the magicians.

Mixing together bits of illusion with stand up comedy, magicians tend to be an interesting lot. Many of them started out by performing tricks for their friends when they were very young and found a way to make a career of it. Most magicians will tell you they enjoy the applause and laughter, but what they especially treasure is that moment when they can make you say, "Now how did they do *that*?" That, my friends, is where the magic is.

Having seen so many of these entertainers up close, I can tell you that it isn't as easy as you might think to make a table disappear, and that you shouldn't try to saw anyone in half without a few lessons. The trick itself, ironically enough, isn't a trick at all – it's just hard work. That is to say, the miracle that you see is the product of hours and years of practice. The illusion is great, but the real magic is making each show better than the one before.

If you're going to continually dazzle your customers, you're going to have to take the same approach. You can't just show up to work and pull a rabbit out of your hat; you're going to have to keep learning and improving. Sadly, though, this is an area where even the best professionals – maybe I should say *especially* the best professionals – lose focus. They get proficient enough with what they're doing that they stop growing. They figure their customers are happy enough, so why worry?

During a recent seminar, I asked my attendees how often they evaluate their own customer service performance to see where they could improve. Only 14% answered that they do so frequently, while 18% admitted that they never have. That means at least one out of five professionals has no idea if they're doing well with their customers or not, and that's out of a group motivated enough to come hear me speak. I wouldn't be surprised if the overall numbers in lots of industries are much lower.

This is no way to get ahead. Learning a customer service system is a great start, and it can put you miles ahead of your peers and competitors. But the key to continuing excellence is to never be satisfied. In the appendix, I've included a helpful survey. Completing it shouldn't take more than a few minutes, and doing so from time to time can help you benchmark your performance.

Another way to get great feedback is by talking to your customers. Find out what their impressions are from working with you. In many cases, your company might routinely survey the men and women with whom you interact. If so, ask to see the results, and study them carefully. You might find an area you can concentrate on improving. Even choosing just one thing to improve each month – answering the phone quickly, learning your customers' names more quickly, or improving your follow-up, for example – can transform your productivity in a very short amount of time.

The superstars in any profession, from sports to retail management, have risen because they're always looking to be the best. They realize that the key to high performance is in small increments, being just a bit better than they were before. Try to think of creative ways to add value for your customers, and after you've done so, try to figure out a way to do it even better the next time. Because in the end, it all comes down to the same thing we started with – *attitude* – and PEOPLE Champions become the best by bringing the right one to work every day.

Something to Think About

I have discovered that when a customer knows you appreciate their business, they give you more.

Excerpted from *High Energy Sales Thoughts: 101 Positive Sales Thoughts and Ideas* by Carl Henry

Why 99% Isn't Enough

In my seminars, often I like to ask people what their customer satisfaction rate is. Usually, I get a number like 75% or 80%. Occasionally, I work with a group that admits to something a bit lower, or boasts something a little higher. But even the most optimistic of them never say they achieve 100%, or even 99%. In fact, most companies would think anything approaching that to be a stellar achievement.

In my opinion though, anything less than 100% still leaves room for improvement. That's because, ideally, every single person who works with you should be happy with the results. Of course, it's hard to please everybody in the real world, but that doesn't mean we should stop trying. And just to keep things in perspective, here's a look at what the world would be like, statistically speaking, if 99.9% were deemed to be 'good enough' in some of our most important industries:

- Two million documents would be lost by the IRS this year.
- 22,000 checks would be deducted from the wrong bank accounts in the next 60 minutes.
- 1,314 phone calls would be misplaced by telecommunication services every minute.
- 12 babies would be given to the wrong parents each day.
- 268,500 defective tires would be shipped this year.
- 14,208 defective PCs would be shipped this year.

- 103,260 income tax returns would be processed incorrectly this year.

- 2,488,200 books would be shipped in the next 12 months with the wrong cover.

- Two plane landings daily at O'Hare International Airport in Chicago would be unsafe.

- 3,065 copies of tomorrow's *Wall Street Journal* would be missing one of the three sections.

- 18,322 pieces of mail would be mishandled in the next hour.

- 291 pacemaker operations would be performed incorrectly this year.

- 880,000 credit cards in circulation would turn out to have incorrect card holder information on their magnetic strips.

- 55 malfunctioning automatic teller machines would be installed in the next 12 months.

- 20,000 incorrect drug prescriptions would be written in the next 12 months.

- 114,500 mismatched pairs of shoes would be shipped this year.

- 107 incorrect medical procedures would be performed by the end of the day today.

- 315 entries in *Webster's Third New International Dictionary of the English Language* would turn out to be misspelled.

A breakdown in communications causes most customer service problems.

CHAPTER NINE
PUTTING THE PEOPLE SYSTEM TO WORK

The PEOPLE Customer Service System can do a lot for you and your company, but only if you're willing to put in the effort. Reading this book, or going to one of my seminars, is never going to be enough. To really get the benefit, you have to take these concepts and make them your own.

With that in mind, I would like to offer you some tips for getting the most out of these pages. None of them center on any specific part of the process, or require that you study other books or materials. They're simply ideas that will help you put PEOPLE to work in the real world.

Learn the Action Guides

As I explained in the beginning of the book, I chose the word PEOPLE for this program because it works out very well as an acronym, and because I wanted my attendees and readers to remember where their focus should remain at all times. But the true value of this approach, what makes it work so well for you and your customers, is that it guides you through your interactions with internal and external customers smoothly, ensuring that you cover all the bases and exceed their expectations.

With that in mind, it's not really the word PEOPLE at all, but the action guides for each chapter, that make everything come together. They're the real meat of the system, and if you want to get the most out of it, you'll need to learn them inside and out. To that end, I recommend you place a copy of your pocket card with the steps and action guides somewhere you can see it while you're on the phone or meeting with clients. It might feel awkward at first, but after a couple of weeks you'll find you know the steps by heart. Once you do, you'll be able to go through them quickly and naturally.

If you need another easy-to-read copy of the steps, simply contact me at chenry@carlhenry.com. I'll be happy to e-mail you printable copies of the pocket cards I give out in my seminar, as well as other information related to The PEOPLE System.

Repetition is Everything

The only way to get really good at customer service, or anything else, is through lots of hard work and repetition. This means you have to start out at the beginning, where things are toughest and you constantly have to remind yourself of what you're doing and why, and keep at it until everything becomes second nature.

The good news, though, is that it probably won't take nearly as long as you think. Psychologists have determined that it only takes three weeks to develop a new habit. So if you take the advice in this book to heart, you could be well on your way to becoming a PEOPLE Champion – and earning the extra income, satisfaction, and job security that affords – a month from now.

Make it as easy on yourself as possible. Set a goal to follow the steps of the system and then keep working on getting better. Pretty soon, you won't just be ahead of your competitors – you'll stay there without even having to try.

Know Your Company's Policies

You've probably noticed that most of the advice found is this book is a bit general – listen carefully here, go above and beyond there, and so on. Part of the reason is because each industry has its own set of common problems and situations. What works for a real estate office might not be a good idea for a clothing company. Besides, your company probably has a set of written policies for dealing with garden variety situations. It's a good idea to know these inside and out, or at least have a good sense of where to find them quickly. Doing things by the book the first time will almost always save you time and embarrassment later.

With that being said, however, remember that policies aren't everything. They're tools put into place to keep things going as smoothly and efficiently as possible. If they get in the way of providing great customer service, then they aren't doing anyone any good. You may come across special cases or situations where the policy doesn't offer the best resolution. Unique and unforeseen problems crop up all the time. If you think a different answer might be best, go with your instinct. And if you don't have the authority to make that call, pass your request along to someone who does. There are few things as pointless as going through the motions, even when you know they won't resolve anything, just because "that's the policy."

Follow your company's procedures, but use common sense. If you find a policy that isn't working, try to change it. Great customer service is all about making people happy, not hiding behind a rule book.

Review and Improve

Getting better at customer service takes time and effort. Pay attention to the feedback that customers and coworkers give you. Do they enjoy interacting with you? Are you making their lives as easy as you could? Are there simple ways you could add value for them? Finding these answers and improving your performance will keep you sharp, and keep you growing as a professional.

Attitude is Everything

All the training and advice in the world won't do anything for you if you don't approach customer service with the right mindset. PEOPLE Champions become who they are because they want to and because they care. They don't hate their jobs, or see their internal and external customers as a burden. Instead, they seem to wake up with the attitude that they're going to exceed expectations if it kills them, and they do.

What I especially want to point out here, though, is that lots of these top performers didn't start out that way. Most of them didn't listen to motivational tapes as toddlers or take customer service classes in college. What they *did* do is make a choice to be the best they can at what they do, and everything else happened as a consequence of that.

That same choice comes to you every morning. Will you grumble in to work and struggle through your day, or will you make the most of your time? Is your job going to be fun and creative, or is it going to be a grueling march against the clock? Everything in this book, all of your potential success, is riding on how you choose to see yourself and those around you.

Do what you can to cultivate a positive attitude. This might mean listening to a few minutes of a positive CD each morning, or choosing to spend time with more upbeat people. It might even be as easy as reminding yourself of who you want to be, or setting a couple of short-term goals. But no matter how you get there, I encourage you to set your attitude in the right direction and keep it there. Happy, positive people aren't just better to their customers – they're better to themselves, too.

Use Time Management and Organizational Skills

Are you always running late? Do you have trouble finding things when you need them? If so, you're probably not doing nearly as well at work as you could be. That's because disorganization creates a vicious cycle. Losing paperwork and information, or constantly being behind schedule, creates a lot of stress and extra work, which naturally leads to more stress and even more work to catch up.

What's more, poor organization will hurt your career. Not only does it make you less effective, but it also damages other people's opinions of you. After all, when you can't manage to be on time, or to clean up your workspace, you're essentially telling other people that you don't care. Even though you have the same number of minutes in a day that they do, you receive the same books and notices, but you can't be bothered to deal with them. So it's only natural that managers and peers, when it's time to look at things like promotions and bonuses, look toward the team members who seem to "have it together."

If you struggle to keep your desk or calendar straight, do yourself a favor and check out a book or course on the topic. A short paperback or weekend seminar won't take more than a couple of hours, but it could have a seismic effect on the way you work and live. I've known lots of people who were able to break bad habits they'd held for decades, just by acknowledging them and deciding to move on. Besides, learning to manage your time and space is another one of those skills that doesn't just pay you back at the office, but at home, too. Everything is less stressful when you don't have to keep one eye on the clock, or move around mountains of clutter.

Don't be a Hermit

In the next chapter, we'll look at the importance of cooperation between departments. But for now, let me just point out that you should make an effort to be involved with the rest of your department and company. Not only will it keep you on top of the latest policies and ideas, but you might learn some things that will make your job easier. From keyboard shortcuts to important telephone numbers and other resources, there are probably dozens of other people looking for the same information you need right now or will require in the future.

Get Good on the Phone

These days, regardless of where you work, much of your interaction with internal and external customers is going to be over the phone. With that in mind, it's critical that you be able to express yourself clearly – and even more importantly, that you can listen for voice inflection and other cues – when you're not speaking in person.

This is one area where a little bit of practice and evaluation can do wonders. It's not a bad idea to record yourself once in a while (with your customer's permission) and then play it back to see how you sound. Pay special attention to things like clarity and tone; make note if you have unconscious habits like sighing or interrupting. Your customers want to feel like you're giving them your undivided personal attention. And if you can make them feel that way, whether you're there in person or not, your interactions with them will resolve much more quickly.

Pick up on Personality Styles

Earlier in the book, I referenced the four major personality styles, and gave each one a color. This was to make them easier to learn and remember, a tactic that's worked well for me. Whenever I meet new customers, I listen closely to what they're saying, and how it's being said, and before too long I can put my finger on it pretty easily: "he's a blue dot," "she's a red dot," and so on.

Cultivating this ability to pick up on personality styles isn't easy, but it gives you a tremendous advantage in customer service and the business world at large. That's because it allows you to communicate with other people on their own terms – to "speak their language" – which is a huge step toward building trust and rapport.

For that reason, take some time to memorize the different styles, along with the best ways to work with each one. By knowing who's who, and which buttons to push or to avoid, you'll be able to reach customers that you might not have been able to connect with before.

Do the Hard Work the First Time

There's an old saying that I think should be posted in every customer service department in the world: "There's never time to do something right, but always time to do it again." As humans, we have a tendency to want to move through things quickly, and to skip steps. Sometimes this comes in the form of recommending solutions to our customers before we fully understand their problems. Other times, it's taking the easy way out and doing a mediocre job instead of doing the dirty work or following a course that takes longer.

I can promise you that it's never worth it to cut corners. Nine times out of ten, it's going to come back to bite you, and whatever you'll have to do to make up for the error will take you twice as long as it would have originally. And even if your internal or external customer doesn't notice, you'll be worried every time they call or visit that they're going to complain. Go easy on yourself and do what you need to the first time.

Don't Over-think Things

Despite all of the thought and work that have gone into making The PEOPLE System as efficient and effective as it can be, there are going to be times when your interaction with a customer is so simple that you won't have to go through very many of the steps. For instance, if a customer walks up to you and asks for a copy of an operating manual or the telephone number for a certain department, your job might be as simple as handing the information over. In the end, PEOPLE is just about doing anything you can to please your internal and external customers. If they give you a very simple way to do that, take it.

Have Fun

One of the easiest ways to be better at your job is just to enjoy doing it. That might seem like a strange concept in our over-worked, stressed-out culture, but it's true. When we're having a good time, we tend to have more energy, get more done, and feel more creative.

Use that information to give yourself permission to have fun. That doesn't mean every day needs to feel like a party, or that work is suddenly going to be a blast. But go out of your way to look for the joy in your job, or at least to find a laugh here and there. There's nothing wrong with reading a joke each morning, or holding a friendly contest with a friend to see who can get the most done. Having fun isn't just more enjoyable, it's also more productive.

Something to Think About

It only takes one

to bring down your whole team

Excerpted from *52 Things Every Sales Manager Needs to Know* by Carl Henry

Great customer service
   providers have the authority
  to make on the spot decisions.

CHAPTER TEN
PEOPLE FOR MANAGERS

After teaching the PEOPLE program for years, I can tell you without a doubt that when it comes to implementing the system, leadership needs to come from the top. Individual members of your team might get it and step up their efforts, but if the managers and supervisors aren't on board, you're never going to get very far. So if you're a manager looking to get better service for and from your internal customers, you're going to have to pave the way.

It usually won't take very long for your staff to find out how serious you are. I sometimes visit companies where the ongoing commitment to customer service is demonstrated by a single seminar every ten years or so. The next day, it's back to business as usual, and the people in charge never breathe another word about it. How much impact do you think any training will have in that environment?

Contrast that with those groups that make service a priority. After our seminar, department heads and other leaders make a small, daily effort to reinforce the material – taking a few minutes here and there to talk about the steps of the system and find out how it's working on the front lines. These companies get a lot more mileage out of my work, because they understand that training is like exercise – you can't do it all at once. It takes consistent effort to make a difference.

And if you aren't the one initiating that effort, then chances are no one else will. Managers are so important because they're the catalysts that transform PEOPLE from a set of ideas and advice into impactful behavioral and operational changes. In other words, your team will never follow if you don't lead. With that in mind, here are some ways managers can get more from the lessons in this book.

Reinforce the System

As I said, simply having a seminar or giving out copies of a book is never going to effect real change. To make a real difference, you're going to have to go over the material with your team from time to time, especially in the beginning.

If you or your staff is new to PEOPLE, then I recommend taking a few minutes with them each morning to go over some of the main aspects. Make sure they understand how to use the steps, and why. Review ways of picking up on personality styles, cultivating stronger listening habits, working on phone skills, and so on. After a couple of months, you'll notice an enormous difference in the way your team works with their internal and external customers.

Once you're sure they grasp the focus of the system and how it works, try to reinforce the finer points at regular intervals, like once a week during a morning meeting. You don't have to go to a lot of effort. Simply pick out one of the action guides and open a discussion about what has been working, or how different people have implemented it. The key is to keep everyone thinking about providing great service, and to make sure they remember the tools they have available to do so.

Speak the Language

A great way to get some extra repetition with PEOPLE is to have your staff talk about their interactions with customers in those terms. In other words, get them to talk, whether it's to you or amongst themselves, about how well they're Engaging, Organizing, etc. Doing so will not only serve as a subtle reminder of their training, but it will help the whole program become second nature, and that's where the real improvement lies.

Keep Your Eyes on the Road

The best managers I know are those who tend to remind their people from time to time that the purpose of the company is to serve internal and external customers. Without customers and teammates, there is no organization. If no one does business with you, then there won't be any more paychecks, bonuses, or promotions. By keeping your focus on that fact – and making sure your team does, too – you go a long way toward setting the stage for five-star service.

You Get What You Reward

Suppose a customer calls your department because there's been a problem with his or her order. Some part of the delivery didn't work correctly, and now the delay has caused a bottleneck in the office or factory. One of your employees, looking to make things right and exceed expectations, decides to track down a new part and have it sent via overnight courier. What would your immediate reaction be?

If your first thought would be to recognize them for a job well done, then it's very likely that your staff will look to go above and beyond in the future. But if you decide to scold them for spending so much on shipping, that message will also carry weight. In fact, it will speak more loudly than anything else you can say about service.

As a manager, it's critical that you understand this point: the behavior that you reward – be it with money, recognition, or in other ways – is the behavior that you can expect in the future. So think carefully about what you really want your staff to do, and then make sure you point it out when you find them doing it.

Take the Long View

Along those same lines, I would like to spend just a moment looking at cost versus value. All too often I see managers lose the forest for the trees by focusing too tightly on daily or weekly budgets. In an effort to control spending, they're sometimes a bit too quick to offer the customer less value than they should.

The problem here is that this strategy always makes sense in the short term, but rarely pays off over time. A satisfied customer, one who will buy from you again and again for years to come, is worth more than the margin on any one sale or quarterly account. Not only do they represent future income, but also a supply of goodwill that isn't easily replaced.

This isn't to say that you want to be foolish about how your department spends money. But when looking at prospective solutions to a customer's problem, think beyond your daily balance sheet. Ask yourself: is there something more I could do here that would earn us a loyal customer for many years to come? If the answer is yes, exercise your common sense instead of reaching for the calculator. It might be harder to do now, but you'll always be glad later.

Empower Employees

At the risk of giving you a shock, I'm going to let you in on a secret: humans aren't perfect, and your employees are going to make mistakes. Other times, though, they're able to blow you away with the thoughtfulness and creativity with which they invent solutions to various problems. How well you handle those mistakes, and how much freedom you give, is going to say a lot about how often they exceed your expectations.

If you want the very best results, you have to allow a certain amount of freedom. People have to know what you want them to do, and then have the flexibility to make it happen in the most efficient way possible. Not only that, but they'll usually do a better job than they would if they were micromanaged. For example, one of my clients empowers his employees to give away anything up to $200 to make a customer happy or resolve a bad situation.

In the past, they were only authorized to issue refunds, credits, and products for a tenth of that amount. So how did they handle the change? Well, the frontline workers, feeling that they're valued and trusted, rarely give away the company's money. What's more, they don't have to bother their supervisor nearly as often as they did before. About every quarter, each member reviews the amounts granted with a supervisor, and works on ways to stick within company guidelines. All in all, the whole department spends less than it ever did, with a lot less management.

Empowering employees isn't just about dollar limits or discounts – it's about teaching them to handle small problems themselves. Once they can, you won't just have a happier staff, you'll have more time for the things that really matter in your business.

Assess Your Team

The world is full of consumer reports. No matter what you want to purchase, someone out there has probably studied it to death. There are literally thousands of magazines and web pages devoted to helping you find the best camcorder, used car, or any other product. And for buyers, it makes great sense. Nobody wants to spend their hard-earned money on something that doesn't work like it should.

And yet I'm constantly surprised at how many managers hire new personnel without running a personality assessment first. Psychologists have shown us repeatedly that there are certain predominant qualities that all of us have, and that some of these are more suited to certain jobs than others. It's not an exact science, of course, but basic assessments can usually determine how likely someone is to succeed in their prospective position. So why not spend a few dollars to find out if you've got the right person for the opening, or if you might be better served interviewing a few more?

If you or your company aren't in the habit of assessing prospective new hires, I would encourage you to try it out for a few months and see if it doesn't make a huge difference. Hiring mistakes are tremendously expensive, and I've never had a single client feel they didn't get their money's worth several times over. You can get more information on customer service assessments by contacting me at chenry@carlhenry.com.

Know When to Critique

There's no way around it – when you're the one in charge, you're going to have to take people to task once in a while. It might be that their work isn't as sharp as it could be, or that they aren't giving their maximum effort. But regardless of the reason, try to make your criticisms into teaching opportunities as much as possible. In every error lies the chance to learn something or make a valuable point. By keeping things focused in that direction, you can stress improvement over reprimands.

Leverage Goodwill

As a leader, it's important that you let people know when they're doing a good job. I've seen managers who were masters at this, and the difference it makes in morale and appreciation is incredible. When your staff knows that you're paying attention to what they do and not just looking for opportunities to criticize them, they'll be a lot more open to your encouragement. Besides, recognition is contagious. Pointing out great work has a two-fold effect: on the one hand, it makes everybody want to do something and stand out, and on the other hand, it gets everyone in the habit of noticing all the good things that are going on. As a manager, that's the best possible result – a great outcome that encourages more great outcomes. So, make a point of catching employees doing something well.

Extend that attitude past your own walls, too. Pass on compliments and recognition to other departments. The same dynamic applies to people who don't work directly under you. Making them feel appreciated can only help their impression of you and your department, not to mention bringing better service in the future.

Something to Think About

Make sure everyone on your staff knows you're there to serve the client

Excerpted from *52 Things Every Sales Manager Needs to Know* by Carl Henry

> *For any group to get beyond mediocre success, they need to get beyond mediocre cooperation first.*

BONUS CHAPTER
BREAKING DOWN WALLS

To understand why some companies have such low internal cooperation, you need only go to a ballgame. It doesn't matter what the sport is, or in what city. Once the game begins, you'll see a large crowd, often decked out in the same reds, blues, and other multicolored jerseys, cheer and boo together as the contest takes shape. Without any sort of prompting, they'll smile at, hug, and high-five each other, all because they happen to be fans of the same team.

Now contrast that with the way many of these same people treat their coworkers on a given day. For most of them, it doesn't even come close; not a lot of people work in offices or production floors where giant foam fingers and group chants are the norm. But putting the issue of what kinds of drinks they serve at the game aside, how can we explain this disparity? Why is it that they will bond with strangers they hardly know, but don't want to be bothered by other employees with whom they're interdependent for things like food and income?

Most people would point to the jovial atmosphere at the

stadium, or the fact that nearly everybody at the game is enjoying their time off. For me, though, the real answer is in what they can see at the game, as compared to what they can't see in their places of business.

Even though most people's office or facility isn't anywhere near the size of a modern sports complex, with its thousands of seats and acres of parking, they can still *see* most of the other fans inside. There are loads of other people supporting the same cause, right before their very eyes. Contrast that with even the smallest office complex. Even if most of the offices are occupied by the same firm (a rarity), they're usually divided by floors, walls, atriums, and elevators. Suddenly, the closest 'fans' outside your department aren't just over in the next row. They're in an office across the hall or, worse yet, in a different building – a virtual world away. Instead of being faces, they're simply voices on the phone or names in an e-mail. Is it any wonder, then, that it's harder to think of them as being close comrades than it is distant strangers?

The bigger the organization, the more prevalent this problem usually becomes. In very small offices, everyone knows what's going on. Each member of the team, from the president to the receptionist, interacts with each other. Consequently, they share the wins and suffer the defeats together. An office party is for everyone, and a bad day is felt from the front door to the back. Even in mid-sized companies, where operations are centered in a single city or area, there tends to remain a feeling of *esprit de corps*. Even if one employee doesn't know another, they usually have a friend, supervisor, or other contact in common. This helps to reduce the perceived space between them. Even distant cousins usually treat each other cordially.

But the biggest companies risk becoming victims of their own success. As they grow and grow, operations spread out over several divisions, headquarters, and business units. There's so much going on that bigger management structures are needed to keep a grip on it all. And in truth, to run a large organization – especially a billion dollar multinational corporation – any other way wouldn't be feasible. But with each of these groups, the interactions become smaller and smaller. The number of people whom each employee knows shrinks, as does their loyalty.

If you think back to our ballgame, each event begins with the crowd singing the national anthem and cheering on the players together. They're conditioned from the outset to see themselves as one, united in a single cause, however frivolous it might be. In small corporate departments, though, things don't work that way. Meetings are held in-house. Memos circulate around the office, but rarely any further. And when directives do come from senior management, they feel like marching orders from a detached leadership. In short, employees are given reason to feel like they're alone, working against the other parts of the company, and so they start to feel that way.

For any organization to achieve real customer service improvement that goes beyond a handful of individuals, this attitude needs to be removed. That's why I'm fond of telling people that if a company is going to grow and thrive, it needs to knock down walls. There cannot be huge mental divides between each person and department. Even if the separate pieces aren't located near each other physically, managers and leadership need to do everything possible to ensure other teams don't feel like strangers and competitors. They need to bring everyone into the stadium – metaphorically speaking – and onto the same page.

Every once in a while, I run across a manager or executive who hears me talk about the need for large organizations to work together. "That's all well and great," they tell me, "but I would rather spend our money on new product development or some other tangible program than just spend it improving our culture. As long as everybody shows up and does their job, we shouldn't have too many problems."

On the surface, I can appreciate that sentiment. The problem, though, is that it's terribly shortsighted. On the one hand, a poor or uncooperative culture will cost you money. When different areas of the company don't work well together, everything takes longer. What's more, burnout is higher, and so is turnover. We've already looked at how much more it costs to bring in a new customer than it does to service an existing one; the same can be said of good employees. When you lose people who know how to do their jobs, between employment ads, interviews, travel costs, and background checks you typically spend thousands trying to replace them.

That's to say nothing of the spillover effect to your external customers. When employees treat each other badly, they're also doing a disservice to the people who buy from you. There's a well-known concept called "six degrees of separation." Basically, it says that no person is ever further than six relationships from any other person on the planet. The idea lends itself to some interesting exercises, but for our purposes, let me just say that when it comes to linking any member of an organization to an external customer, it's hardly ever more than one or two. That is, if you don't deal directly with customers, you almost always deal with someone who is. And you're never much farther away than that.

When the departments of companies stop cooperating, the tension never stays in-house. As coworkers stop trying to exceed, or even meet, each others' expectations, satisfaction drops. The customer waits longer for a call back, the new part shows up more slowly than it should. Even if they can't tell the exact cause of their poor treatment, customers figure out that something is wrong. Naturally, they do what they can to stay away. At first, they may just feel less satisfied with their service. But over time, they will almost always look for a new supplier.

With that in mind, it's easy to see why we have to work so hard to integrate all the parts of the organization. There's no company around that can afford the costs – from higher turnover to lower customer retention – that come with a group that doesn't work well together. The key is to take the barriers away.

How do we knock down walls? The easiest and fastest way is by using that hammer we call interaction. That is, people from different departments need to see each other. They don't have to do it every day, or even all that often, but it's critical that they can put at least a few faces with names.

Cross training different departments is an idea that I wholeheartedly recommend. I don't mean that in the sense that every person should be able to do everyone else's job, but that each member of the company occasionally spends a day or two working alongside someone from a different department, seeing what goes on there. Such exercises can put your group light years ahead when it comes to cooperation and efficiency. For one thing, it helps with the problem we looked at a moment ago, where no one knows anyone else. At the same time, it also makes people more proficient in their own jobs. If the human resources person, for example, learns a little bit about technical support, it might carry over into her own habits and work area, which can save everyone time and money. The real benefit, though, comes in understanding. To understand someone, you really do have to walk a mile in their shoes. And often, once you have, it permanently changes the way you see and treat them.

I've seen this happen first-hand on countless occasions. In one instance, a sales rep was spending time with an accounting department manager. There had been some friction between the two areas, as the salespeople were always trying to get completed quotes and terms from the accounting team, who in return wanted complete project specs. By simply spending a couple of hours together, and having the sales rep see how the estimates were formulated while explaining his interactions with the customer, both sides quickly were able to realize how they might be able to help each other. Best of all, they took that information back to their respective departments. Now, not only did they know how to get things done more quickly and with less hassle, but the whole tone of the interaction had changed. The meeting had reminded them of what they already knew – that they were on the same team, working together toward the same goals.

In a similar situation, I saw how cooperation between a production line and customer service department improved through a basic morning workshop. By just having the two groups in the same room for a couple of hours talking about their biggest challenges, they were able to find a new appreciation for the teamwork they needed. It's important to note that each of these meetings was short and largely informal. There were no heavy agendas, and no one invented a new product or revolutionized the company's way of doing things. But these small interactions and the familiarity they afford can save a company millions of dollars over the long run.

In the same way, there are a lot of other activities that can help bridge the gap between different departments. Typically, they are the first things to be cut when a market or economy goes bad – things like birthday parties, pizza lunches, softball games, and so on. None of these, in and of themselves, is going to solve a morale problem within your organization. But together, they act as a kind of oil to your cultural engine, keeping people synchronized and working well together.

This isn't to say that every company, especially those facing dire straits, should go overboard with celebrations and social gatherings. I do want to make the point, however, that they're often removed from the budget without any serious thought to the long-term effects. Little things go a long way. Each time a number of individuals from the company get together outside of their normal routine – and especially outside of their everyday circle – they bring back a bit of perspective. And each time they get a chance to look at another person or department in a new light, the multiplying effect of that change goes from one employee to another.

The PEOPLE Customer Service System can help you immeasurably in your own career and department. But if you want to spread things even farther, you'll have to knock down some walls. You don't have to spend a lot of time or money to do it, but whatever effort you do put out there will repay you a dozen times over.

Something to Think About

You have to have

You can't prosper in this job unless you truly enjoy it.

Excerpted from *High Energy Sales Thoughts: 101 Positive Sales Thoughts and Ideas* by Carl Henry

APPENDIX

In order to truly master The PEOPLE Approach to Customer Service, you have to work to continually get better. Time and again, I've seen that the top performers - that is, the companies and individuals that enjoy the greater profits and loyalty that come with happier customers - get that way because they're continually refining their approach.

Towards that end, I've included a set of surveys that I give out to my seminar attendees. In each of them, you'll find a handful of questions specifically designed to help you think about what kind of service you're *really* providing to your internal and external customers.

Take some time once a week, or even once a quarter, and see how you stack up. Notice if your attitudes or behaviors change over time, as this can clue you in on your own progress, or help you to recognize areas where you could improve.

Remember, when you're dealing with your customers - the lifeblood of your business and career - there's no such thing as 'good enough,' and those who are willing to work at their craft are the ones who will reap the biggest rewards.

PEOPLE Approach
Customer Service Awareness Survey

PREPARE FOR YOUR INTERNAL & EXTERNAL CUSTOMERS	Not Applicable	Never	Seldom	Sometimes	Usually	Always
1. I understand my customer is the most important person in business.						
2. My goal for customer service is 100% (internal and external) customer satisfaction.						
3. I have a pro-active champion attitude toward customer service.						
4. I have a sense of urgency when encountering my customer.						
5. I prepare in advance for my customer whenever possible.						
6. I use eye contact when listening to my customer.						
7. I project my voice clearly when communicating.						
8. I have a good ability to really listen and hear another person.						

PEOPLE Approach
Customer Service Awareness Survey

ENGAGE YOUR INTERNAL & EXTERNAL CUSTOMERS	Not Applicable	Never	Seldom	Sometimes	Usually	Always
1. I use my customer's name when speaking to him/her.						
2. I remember my role in solving my customer's problem.						
3. I focus on my customer regardless of outside events.						
4. I take responsibility for having a favorable encounter with my customer.						
5. I instill confidence in my customer.						
6. I make my customer feel comfortable.						
7. I quickly adapt myself to other people's personality styles.						
8. I can recognize other personality styles easily.						

PEOPLE Approach
Customer Service Awareness Survey

ORGANIZE YOUR INTERNAL & EXTERNAL CUSTOMER'S NEEDS	Not Applicable	Never	Seldom	Sometimes	Usually	Always
1. I am aware of the importance of asking needs and wants questions.						
2. I am good at asking needs and wants questions at the appropriate time.						
3. I comfortably ask for clarification if I am unclear of my customer's answer.						
4. I mentally prepare questions in advance of serving my customer.						
5. I ask more open-ended, needs development questions than yes-no questions.						
6. I verify that my understanding of my customer's needs and wants is accurate.						
7. I try to recommend the best solution to my customer's problem.						
8. I make it easy for my customer to communicate his/her problems.						

PEOPLE Approach
Customer Service Awareness Survey

PERFORM QUALITY SERVICE	Not Applicable	Never	Seldom	Sometimes	Usually	Always
1. I am aware of the importance of delivering promised services to my customer.						
2. I go out of my way to reassure my customer I am honored to solve their problems.						
3. I build trust with my customer by delivering promised service promptly.						
4. I check to make sure my customer is satisfied with the delivered service.						
5. I try to solve unresolved problems by getting customer feedback.						
6. I display a positive attitude while working with a dissatisfied customer.						
7. I understand the quality of service I deliver internally ultimately affects the external customer's satisfaction.						
8. I go the extra mile to keep my customer informed.						

PEOPLE Approach
Customer Service Awareness Survey

LEVERAGE YOUR INTERNAL & EXTERNAL CUSTOMER'S GOODWILL	Not Applicable	Never	Seldom	Sometimes	Usually	Always
1. I understand the concept of leveraging my customer's goodwill.						
2. I encourage my customer to pass on positive feedback about the service performed.						
3. If appropriate, I offer additional service.						
4. I realize my relationship with both internal and external customers affect my company's success.						
5. I promote my company in a positive manner.						
6. If my internal or external customer exhibits extreme satisfaction, I encourage them to pass on their goodwill to others.						
7. I try to build a long term relationship between my company and my customer.						
8. I feedback important information to my company that will help service our customers better in the future.						

PEOPLE Approach
Customer Service Awareness Survey

EXCEED YOUR INTERNAL & EXTERNAL CUSTOMER'S EXPECTATIONS	Not Applicable	Never	Seldom	Sometimes	Usually	Always
1. I try to find unique ways to exceed both my internal and external customer's expectations.						
2. I execute my ideas for exceeding my customer's expectations as quickly as possible.						
3. I do not let barriers prevent me from exceeding my customer's expectations.						
4. I insure my ideas for extra value are applicable to my customer.						
5. I critique my people skills on a regular basis.						
6. I leave my customer with a desire to maintain and strengthen their relationship with my company.						
7. I consciously look for ways to expand my mental customer care paradigm.						
8. I realize exceeding my customer's expectations positions me as a highly valuable professional.						

Carl Henry is a sales educator, keynote speaker and corporate consultant. During the course of his own successful career, he developed The MODERN Sales System, which he has been sharing with companies and associations around the world for many years.

A Certified Speaking Professional and a member of the National Speakers Association, Carl teaches essential sales skills with humor, insight and personal experience. Hundreds of companies throughout a diverse range of industries have used his highly-acclaimed seminars to educate and inspire their sales teams.

Carl's other books include The MODERN Sales System, The PEOPLE Approach to Customer Service and 15 Hot Tips that Will Supercharge Your Sales Career.

He currently lives in Charlotte, North Carolina.

To order additional copies of this book, or find out about Carl's seminars contact him at:

Henry Associates
704-847-7390
9430 Valley Road Charlotte, NC 28270
chenry@carlhenry.com
www.carlhenry.com

To order additional copies of this book contact:

Henry Associates
704-847-7390
9430 Valley Road Charlotte, NC 28270
chenry@carlhenry.com
www.carlhenry.com

Printed in the United States
125822LV00001B/1-192/P